THE CALL OF
STEAM

To Jane Again,
and Britain's railway men

THE CALL OF
STEAM

ROBERT ADLEY

'But now will canker sorrow eat my bud,
And chase the native beauty from his cheek.
And he will look as hollow as a ghost
As dim and meagre as an ague's fit;
And so he'll die.'

King John
Act III Scene IV

Bounty Books

First published in Great Britain in 1982 by
Blandford Press

This edition published 2005 by Bounty Books,
a division of Octopus Publishing Group Ltd
2–4 Heron Quays, London E14 4JP

ISBN 0 7537 1065 X
ISBN13 9780753710654

A CIP catalogue record for this book is available from the British Library

Printed and bound in China

Contents

Introduction

PLATE 1. From 'Now' to 'Then' and the cold midwinter of January 1963. The icy grip of a future without steam, seems somehow portended by LMS '4F' 0–6–0 No. 44269 clattering over the pointwork at the western approach to Bristol Temple Meads station on the 23rd of that Arctic month. The LMS was never better personified than by the '4F': soon the faceless diesel will eliminate the variety so visibly expressed at Temple Meads by the two company's locomotives, at this great tribal meeting place of LMS and GWR. Such a humble scene as this personifies the magic that was the working steam railway.

Politicians suffer from verbal diarrhoea, so writing introductions to books should be simple enough. Railway enthusiasts are not always noted for the conciseness or abruptness of their conversation, either. Thus the opening section of this book may not, perhaps qualify the writer for a prize for brevity. In truth however I am writing this, and you are reading it, not for educational but for recreational pursuit. As this is the third introduction with which I have commenced a railway book, my theme is to capitalise upon the comments contained in correspondence on my previous efforts. Let me try to do just that.

Firstly, a lot of people *have* written to me. Secondly they have, without exception, been kind, even effusive. Thirdly, it seems that the memories evoked by *In Search of Steam* have stirred recollections in the hearts of the writers, many of whom have sought to share with me fond remembrances of the steam era. Little did I imagine that my reference to the 4.25 Salford to Colne express would have brought a letter from a civil engineer, born and brought up in Bolton who writes 'We often saw the 4.25 Salford–Colne express awaiting departure from Salford ...'. A correspondent from Fort William comments on two photographs that caught his eye. Kindly describing them as First Class (*sic*) he says they are 'two pictures I have never seen before, no doubt because it is a very unlikely place to go trespassing.'

It is not only hearts that are stirred by railway memories. In the caption to one of the photographs in *In Search of Steam*, I pondered the reason why a particular GWR 'Hall' had been at Birkenhead on a particular date. You may imagine the pleasure with which I received the following letter from Mr R. W. Fletcher of Codsall, near Wolverhampton:

'I have just purchased and enjoyed your book, *In Search of Steam 1962–68*. On page 123 plate 55, which shows 7924 Thornycroft Hall on Birkenhead shed on the 11 July 1965. Which was on a Sunday. On Saturday 10th July 1965 at Wolverhampton

Low Level 7924 came through the station on a passenger train at about 1.35 p.m. heading towards Shrewsbury. I hope this information is any help to you. I look forward to your next book which I hope will be of the same high standard as the others.'

If people are reading my efforts that carefully, I have presumed that the formula to be followed this time should not be altered too drastically. The critics have been kind, too. However, one journal found the two poems in *In Search of Steam* somewhat less than unforgettable: indeed my wife Jane described them as 'the worst poetry written in England this century'. But she does not read much poetry.

Inevitably one is swamped with questions as to wherein lies the fascination of the steam railway. The answer can only be found in the heart and mind of the individual enthusiast. Tangibly, the sheer manifestation of power and movement, latent and actual strength, visual partnership between man and machine created in his own image, and the harnessing of natural resources to serve man's basic needs, accounts for appreciation of the steam engine. Yet that is but half the story. The steam age bred men of style. The railway fashioned our economy, our geography and indeed our history. The passing of the steam era has in no way diminished its appeal, as is evidenced by the preservation era. Indeed we are witnessing the creation of a new form of archaeology: railway archaeology. Its study offers seeds of a new educational experience; the study of places of fame and distinction in the railway era, whose significance should not, indeed must not be allowed to pass into oblivion.

I have tried, in this book, to call to mind places with a rightful claim to fame in railway history: places where once were sited important junctions, great marshalling yards, fine station buildings. How careless we are of our history. Why did we allow thousands of miles of railway line to be destroyed? To discontinue service may have been an economic necessity; to destroy the basic infrastructure upon which that service was provided, is less understandable. What value judgement seeks to designate the Firestone Tyre Factory as of architectural merit, yet fails to recognise the value of Ribblehead Viaduct? Why should we expect British Rail to pay for the upkeep of some of Britain's finest monuments to our forebear's energy, bravery and ingenuity, and then chastise them if they cannot make ends meet? Whom shall we criticise for the constant cost of repairs to our motorways? Whose balance sheet, other than the Government's, must bear the cost of workmanship by modern engineers whom Locke & Stephenson would never have employed?

So much for politics! What is this Call of Steam? Where shall I recommend you to go in order to savour it to the full. Why not try

8

Woodford Halse? If space permitted I should love to write a whole chapter about that place. Tramping the long-deserted track-beds where railway lines once threaded our countryside, brings strange rewards. Go to Midhurst. Seek out the boarded-up tunnels. Collect the odd bits of metal still to be found, buried deep in the undergrowth. I found three lumps of coal quite recently; just by the entrance to Cocking Tunnel on the LBSCR line from Midhurst to Chichester. If I were a school master I should set a thesis for my pupils 'With pencil, paper and camera, recreate the Waverley Route'.

Now there is a name with which to conjure! Hills and dales: moors and remote villages: border country twixt Scotland and England: branch lines from nowhere to nowhere: rivers and bridges: the Waverley must have been marvellous. How dare I presume to mention it. How poor is my memory of steam, for lack of knowing, it. Am I odd in finding fascination amongst the remote emptiness of Britain's landscape? Who cannot be mesmerized by Rannoch Moor?

I feel no need to apologise for my mental and physical attachment to Scotland. Not even two weeks incessant rain on the flat featureless island of Tiree some years ago, has dissipated the charm. The fierce battles that raged between the Caledonian Railway (Caley) and the North British Railway (NBR) are legendary to students of Scotland's railway history. Whilst Scotland, like England, has seen so many lines run down, closed, overgrown and recorded only as 'course of old railway' on the Ordnance Survey Maps, some lines have happily survived, albeit of course diesel-operated and deprived of character, glamour and spirit. One of these survivors is the Glasgow & South Western Railway (G & SW) line from Stranraer to Glasgow; I was determined to visit the line.

You need to ride the footplate fully to appreciate the Swan's Neck. Of all the many lines in Britain that I never saw in steam, the Stranraer Road of the old G & SW tugged most vigorously at my imagination, yet resisted most strongly all attempts to provide me with the opportunity to sample. At last, however, my moment came. On Thursday, 6 August, 1981, I stepped aboard the 07.27 Stranraer to Glasgow Central Train. My ambition was fulfilled, and gloriously, too, thanks to two fine men of steam.

The G & SW, or at least the Stranraer Road, is spiritually a northern S & DJ, combining charm and challenge to enginemen and the operating department. With much at stake that Thursday morning I sought the driver on Stranraer station. The porter told me who was on, and helpfully took me down the platform, to the door marked 'Inspectors Office' in fading Scottish Region blue. Inside the office sat two men: the one nearer the door gave an early-morning grunt in response to my cheekily chirpy 'Excuse me, are you the driver?' My mind was searching speedily for a suitable riposte to the grunt, followed by a quizzical 'What now?' silent, searching look from this craggy individual.

'Are you in a good mood this morning?' was the best I could do – not good enough, surely.

'What do you want?'

'I'm going to Glasgow, and have always wanted to do this run. Could you do with some company in the cab?'

'Aye – all right.'

Thus was I teamed up with James Bradley, 40 years an LMS and BR man at Stranraer. The next couple of hours contained, for me, a satisfying diet of railway history, scenic joy, richness of human character and downright common sense, more agreeable than many of the conversations that life strews in my path.

Half-past-seven in the morning is no time for an English railway enthusiast, who happens to be a Member of Parliament, to prattle loudly to a dour Scot, some 20 years his senior, on his home ground. My gratitude at his willingness to allow me to ride the footplate (ugh-cab) with him, seemed to me to entitle him to silence from his self-invited guest. This gave me time to ponder the dilemma in which I always find myself. Do I tell him I am an MP, and thus perhaps annoy him and make him feel he is being snooped on: or do I say nothing, and have trouble with my conscience that I am deceiving him? My problem was quickly solved, as we received the 'Right Away' from the Guard.

'There are eight men around the station here now. In LMS days there was one. All we've got to show for it is paper, paper, paper.' I resisted the temptation to elaborate on his train of thought about overmanning, centralisation, lack of incentive. Instead I asked him if he knew Derek Cross, whose home at Maybole was on our route. Having minor linguistic problems, recurring through accent rather than vocabulary, my comment that Derek was a farmer led him to ask me one or two odd questions, only sorted out when I realised that he thought I had said that Derek was my father!

As we pulled away from Stranraer I cleaned the lens of my camera. With Driver James Bradley's help, I hoped to photograph some of the line's landmarks from the cab. It was early morning, we were on the move, and the light was none too good, but the line immortalised by David Smith in *Legends of the Glasgow and South Western Railway* presented for me a more exciting journey than those featured in the glossy travel agents' brochures. Of course, the motive power was merely boring; that journey on the footplate of a swaying, bucking, heaving steam locomotive must have been an unforgettable experience. Yet, as we gathered speed, left Stranraer and the urban world behind, and headed into the open country, passing the site of Dunragit Station I scanned the landscape ahead for the first significant landmark – if landmark there would be. My aim was to find the remains of Challoch Junction, where the GSWR main line to Girvan, Ayr and Glasgow bore away to the north, parting company from what must have been one of Britain's most attractive cross-country railways, the Portpatrick and Wigtownshire Joint (PPW).

By now you must be wondering what I am going on about! My book is entitled 'The Call of Steam': I am in the cab of a diesel: and starting to reminisce about a railway line that no longer exists and which I never even knew. My explanation lies in the belief that the steam engine opened up Britain: construction of the lines generated not just employment and prosperity, but created completely new communities and ways of life. Therein lies the breadth of interest in railways like the PPW, for it was the steam engine that created the railway systems of Britain: and the recognition of its revolutionary transport potential that sparked off enthusiasm for the Portpatrick Railway, amongst innumerable others. What must have been a delightful cross-country railway is now little more than a scar across the landscape, more of interest to archaeologists perhaps than to students of transport. Bridges and embankments will survive for many years, for our railway forebears built to last. The call of the railway is almost synonymous with the call of steam, for the birth of our railways was itself synonymous with the dawn of the steam age. The early railway engineers worked with the landscape, in harmony not in conflict. If readers of this Introduction can be enrolled into the ranks of steam enthusiasm, and into an appreciation of the archaeological value of our railway lines, then I can feel that I may have achieved new allies for the cause.

These were the thoughts that swirled around my head as James Bradley interrupted my reverie. 'There it is, Challoch Junction, that's the way the Boat Trains used to go.' On a low embankment, the trackbed was clearly visible, as the line from Challoch Junction only closed on 14 June 1965.

Looking subsequently at my photograph of Challoch Junction, taken early on an overcast West of Scotland summer morning, reveals a featureless, even unattractive landscape to the uninformed eye. Yet my note on the transparency as O/S map – 170571 (82) – led to subsequent searches through the Ordnance Survey archives that both satisfy curiosity and justify my claim that an interest in railways is an excellent means of creating an enjoyment of and education in both history and geography. That map reference on the current O/S map shows the railway line from Stranraer turning sharply north, whilst ahead, eastwards on

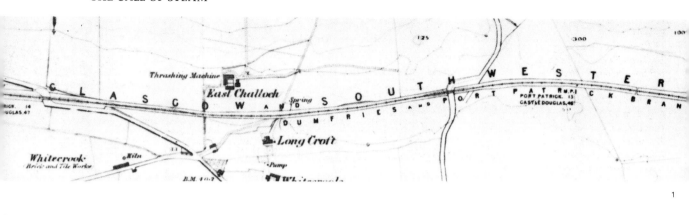

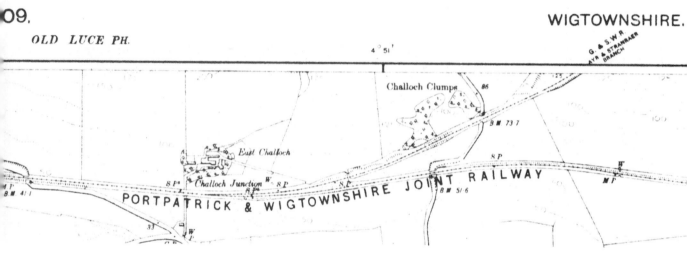

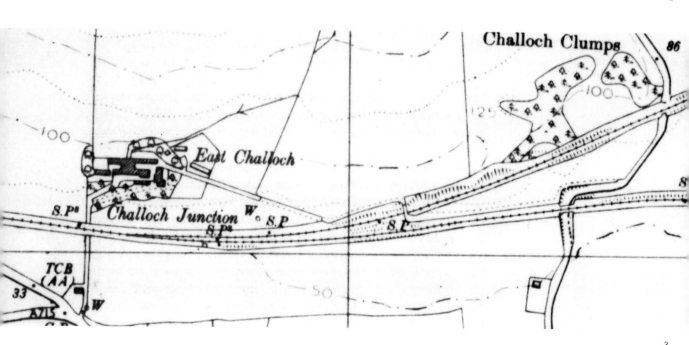

Figs 1, 2 and 3 (page 12) Fig. 4
(page 13)
Challoch Junction. *Four
Ordnance Survey maps that
tell their own tale. In the first,
dated 1847, there is no
Junction at Challoch. The now-
closed Port Road (see Page 18)
runs east-west, noted as
Dumfries and Port Patrick
Branch of the Glasgow &
South Western Railway. The
second map, dated 1906,
shows the Junction, formed by
the G & SWR Ayr & Stranraer
Branch off the Portpatrick and
Wigtownshire Joint Railway.
By the date of the next map,
1957, the Junction is just a
railway landmark in
anonymous Brtish Rail: whilst
finally, the 1978 Ordnance
Survey map shows the wheel
turned full circle. The
Stranraer to Ayr line, junior
partner in the Junction is still
open but the original Port
Road has gone – just another
'track of old railway'.*

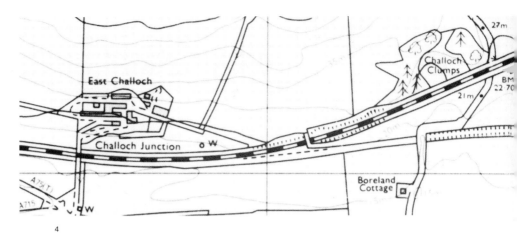

4

the map, lies a dotted line with those depressing words 'course of
old railway'. Yet study of the early Ordnance Survey maps, with
their beautiful printed calligraphy, shows that the 'Port Road'
was built well before the line north from Challoch Junction.

To write in any detail of the old Port Road would be unjustified
here: yet my journey north from Challoch Junction with Driver
Bradley that morning, and the photographs I took, albeit with
steam long gone, may illustrate the interest and pleasure that the
student of railway history can still obtain, if only you can find a
companion who knows the road. My next shot explains it all.
'This is the Swans Neck – you'll want a photograph of this piece
of the line.'

As the morning light improved, we left behind the flatlands
and began to climb into the bleak, sometimes boggy moorland
that would be our scenery for many miles. Here, the railway line
itself was a ribbon of comfort in a lonely landscape. At
Glenwhilly we reached the first crossing loop on the single line.
My photograph of the signal-box shows a tidy building at this
lonely outpost which has lost its railway station. Comparing my
picture with the black-and-white one on page 126 of David
Smith's *Legends of the Glasgow and South Western Railway* the
current level of maintainance appears good. Through Glenwhilly
we kept climbing, and James Bradley began to relate his tales of
the slog to Barrhill Summit in steam days. One did not need much
imagination to envisage the hostility of rain and wind fighting to
prevent the Manson 4–4–0s fulfilling their allotted role, to get
'The Paddy' – the Stranraer Boat-Train – through on time.

Away across the moorland, and Glentrool Forest, the distant
hills – Kirriereoch, Merrick, Benyellary – beckoned me as the
highlands of Scotland always do; not, of course that this is
Highland Scotland, quite the reverse. Soon we were into Barrhill,
on time at 08.08. People! Two railwaymen awaited our arrival,

PLATE 2. The Swans Neck on the Glasgow and South Western Railway.

but no passengers. Again, the station and its immediate environs appeared to be the total community of Barrhill, the village itself out of sight in the valley. I was happy to enjoy the privileged view of the landscape provided for the railway traveller, as well as to listen to my companion's informed commentary of the line's 'why and wherefore'. He allowed me to take his photograph – silhouetted against the passing green scenery. Ere long we were at Pinwherry, another famous point – scene of an awful accident in 1928 when a goods train seemingly out of control, careered down the bank from Barrhill, hurtled through the station which is on a sharp curve, and, at the north end of the loop, rocking wildly, came off the rails. The engine plunged down the bank, turned upside down, and embedded itself in the earth. Twenty-five goods wagons followed: steam enveloped the scene: as the locomotive's wheels stopped spinning, the steam began to clear. Driver and fireman were killed instantly.

As the Pinwherry signalman maintained the link with the past by handing over the staff for the single-line section, James Bradley pointed out to me the house where James Barke wrote about Burns. I reflected on the superior educational system Scotland seems always to have possessed over England – or is it just that railwaymen are more enlightened and rounded

PLATE 3. 'Paddy's Milestone'
– Ailsa Craig, seen from the
footplate.

characters than most of their fellow men?

This is not a book of philosophy, or yet of history or geography save in the railway context. I love our railway system, with its kaleidoscopic variety. By now we were down from the hills, and in sight of the sea. 'There she is – Paddy's Milestone.' As I am writing this Introduction I am as yet unaware if my kind publisher will allow me to include the photograph of Ailsa Craig, lest I stand accused of writing a gazeteer rather than a railway book! Yet in Scotland the railway presents views of hill, loch and sea unsurpassed from the vantage point of the mere motorist. I hope you can see Ailsa Craig: then you may be tempted to ride the Sou' Western to Stranraer, as I did that day.

More photographs followed: Girvan: then we were passing beneath 'Derek Cross's bridge' – at Killochan, from where many a fine photograph was conceived and born. Though Kilkerran is now but a passing loop, we were stopped by flag by the signalman and advised to beware cattle on the road ahead. Then it was Maybole, Dalrymple Junction, and into Ayr. From 07.27 Stranraer, to 09.02 Ayr, was but ninety-five minutes: but enough time to have met a man whose kindness I shall not forget: one of Britain's Railwaymen. We bade farewell at Ayr. Would the new driver allow me to continue my cab ride?

David McGavin was in his thirty-seventh year as a railwayman, all of them based at Glasgow's Polmadie MPD. Both his father and his grandfather, as well as an uncle, had spent their entire working lives at Polmadie. Where else in British industry, indeed in our whole society will you find that depth of tradition still maintained? With the tradition goes the loyalty: but nowadays to the *idea* of railways rather than to the *company*.

Where James Bradley was a countryman, there was less reticence with David McGavin. Seated on his driver's perch he responded briskly and firmly to my questions. Was there a 'call of steam'? The response was swift, certain. 'Now, I'm just a glorified tram driver: in those days it was a different railway, a different class of man.'

In his time at Polmadie he had driven a 'Lizzie', but preferred the 'Scotsman': I reflected, indeed glowed in the bond between us that enabled me, unsaid, to understand his references to the LMS Stanier Pacifics and 'Royal Scot' 4–6–0s. My overt pleasure, as we passed Falkland Junction, at being for the first time at places about which I had heard and read so often, on this particular piece of railway territory, obviously pleased him, and caused him helpfully to point out the numerous railway landmarks hereabouts. Troon Station justifiably merited praise. At Barassie Junction he pointed out the 'link line to Carlisle': in other words, since the closure of the Port Road, the 'most direct' route between Carlisle and Stranraer! *He* understood clearly enough why the previous day, I had had to hire a car to travel between Carlisle and Stranraer, not having half a day to spare to wait for the rare passenger trains going this long way round.

As David McGavin began to reminisce about the relative merits of LMS and LNER engines – 'I didn't like the LNER engines' – I anticipated accurately that he was about to embark on an exposition of the superiority of *his* railway: and so it was to be. The continuation, in the 1980s, of the railway company rivalries of a hundred years ago, remains a source of fascination to me. Indeed, Chapter 5 'The Ghosts of Kinnaber' amplifies the point. Not even the 1923 Grouping: the 1948 Nationalisation: or even the mass closures in the mid-sixties of lines like the Port Road between Dumfries and Stranraer, or the Strathmore Line, between Kinnaber Junction and Stanley Junction, can ever it seems stifle the rivalries or the memories.

It occurs to me that I am writing about a distant land with which you are totally unfamiliar. With assistance from a 'borrowed' copy of British Railways Scottish Region Sectional Appendix to the Working Timetable and Books of Rules and Regulations, I have (with permission) copied their line diagrams of Scotland's current rail network, but added in the 'missing

Fig. 5 (page 17)
Sectional Maps From Current
BR Working Timetable
*The dotted lines indicate the
'missing link' of two famous
former Scottish main lines.
Between Stanley Junction and
Brechin was the Strathmore
Line, once the racing ground of
Glasgow–Aberdeen Expresses.
(opposite)*

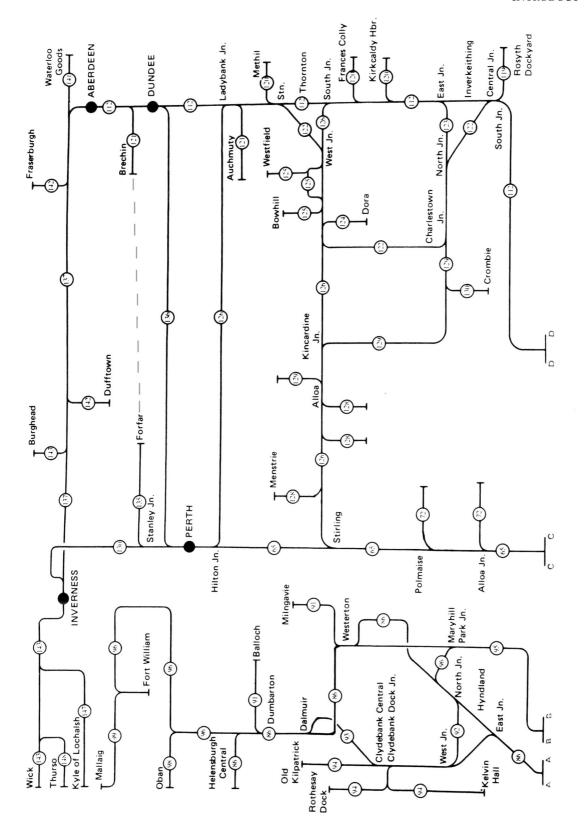

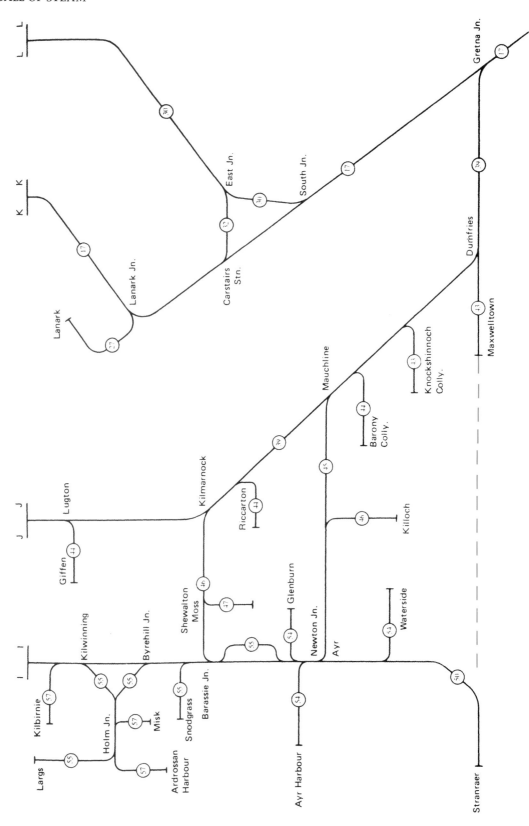

Fig. 6 (page 18)
Between Stranraer & Dumfries was the Port Road, once the main line for the Euston–Stranraer Boat Trains. Extract from Pages 12 and 15 of the Sectional Appendix to the Working Timetable of Books of Rules & Regulations – Scottish Region. (Courtesy BR)

links' to which I have just referred: this hopefully will illustrate my meaning and point.

How many people, even enthusiasts, really realise the depth of knowledge required of the railwayman before he is considered competent to do his job? The Scottish Region's Book of Rules and Regulations is not exceptional. Yet it contains 276 pages of minute yet vital detail of railway operations, most of which is related to safety. How angry I get when the very occasional railway mishap leaps out from the pages of newspapers, when quite probably a handful of people may have been slightly shaken: yet that same day, every day, every week, inexorably, our roads take a constant toll of death and maiming with barely a comment. If road transport had to comply with the railway's safety requirements BR would become the world's most profitable organisation overnight.

Let me finish my journey with David McGavin. At Kilwinning Junction my photograph shows another neat station, trim signal box and pert semaphore signals. Here, by the Ayrshire coast, was battle joined in earnest between the Glasgow and South Western and the Caledonian Railways for the profitable commuter traffic into Glasgow. The Caley passenger line via Auchenmade is no more: indeed, comparative study of the Ian Allan *Pre-Grouping Atlas and Gazeteer* and the Oxford Publishing Company's *Rail Atlas of Britain* is itself an exercise in railway history, particularly illustrative around places like Kilmarnock. There are scores of similar sites, sadly, around Britain.

We were nearing journey's end. At Paisley Gilmour Street I was able only to imagine Whitelegg's huge GSW Baltic Tanks racing the Caley machines over the Glasgow and Paisley Joint (G & P) line to Shields Junction. As the sun shone through the catenaries supporting the overhead electric wires, casting their shadows on Gilmour Street's platforms, my companion himself reminded me of those great competitive days. Shields Junction is still there: St Enoch Station has gone, like many famous city termini (see Chapter 9 'The Train Not Standing at Platform 2'). As we rounded the curve to join what is now the only main line into Glasgow Central from the South, covered by a tangle of overhead electric wires, crossed the Clyde, and came to a halt under that great canopy, the extent to which the development of the railway so affected and dominated the growth and style of the city of Glasgow was brought forcibly to my mind. The passion and drama, intrigue and skulduggery of railway rivalry was nowhere more fierce and frenzied than in the struggles betwixt and between the GSW, the Caley and the North British Railway (NB) for their stations in the city centre. You do not need to ask the House of Commons library for copies of the Committee hearings of the Caledonian Glasgow Central Station Bill, put forward in May 1873, to comprehend the scale and scope of the rivalry. Read instead John Kellett's excellent book *Railways and Victorian Cities*.

So I bade farewell to David McGavin, an unsung descendant of a line of railwaymen whose history seems to me to be inadequately recorded or recognised in our nation's annals. Britain's railway heritage is the richest in the world, yet it lies dormant and unnoticed before our very noses, save only by those few dedicated railway historians. Wearing my 'hat' as Chairman of the Parliamentary Tourism Committee I am trying to rectify this: by seeking greater public interest in the men and of course the buildings that are our legacy. I write these words confronted by an interesting brochure issued by the City of Glasgow District Council: it is called Glasgow (Central) Heritage Trail: but not a mention is there of Glasgow Central! Add to that, split infinitives and a slight political tinge to the copy, and my displeasure is complete.

One facet of this book has been my attempt to satisfy those who have complained of my neglect of their favourite areas, in my previous books. Naturally my ability to encompass a particular location is heavily dependent on the availability of my own photographs – that goes without saying. Nevertheless, by including chapters entitled 'Midlands' and 'Yorkshire' I have managed, inadequately but as best I can, to cover two areas previously neglected. My 'Ghosts of Kinnaber' may seem to be stretching the goodwill of readers whose main interest is captioned coloured photographs of locomotives in BR service between 1962–68. I hope no reader will feel that recounting my visit to Ferryhill MPD, Aberdeen, is inappropriate in *The Call of Steam*.

I make no pretensions to be adding to the sum of human knowledge and experience. My aim is to please. If it is arrogant to say that I enjoyed writing this book, not least for its action in bringing me into intimate contact with more of my photographs, then I can only apologise. The sweet pangs of memory can best be stirred by recollection of personal experience: the chance to share one's own experiences as railway enthusiast and photographer, with sympathetic souls and kindred spirits, is surely justification for my temerity in offering you *The Call of Steam*.

1 Feltham

'Funny place, Feltham: sort of nowhere.' Thus philosophised one of the staff at the shed, to whom I was chatting. Indeed it seemed an unlikely location for a large, important freight motive power depot and marshalling yard. Of all the sheds visited during my frantic search for steam to photograph between 1962 and 1968, I probably made as many visits to, and spent as much time at Feltham as at any other shed. One reason was its proximity to our first and second homes in Chiswick and Sunningdale. The other was my friendship with Shedmaster Ted Richardson.

To those with no interest in railways, and with little time or concern for the lives of those outside their family or occupational circle, railways and trains, if considered at all, are taken for granted. Thoughts about working hours or conditions of those responsible for keeping goods and passengers on the move rarely disturb tranquil hours at office desk, on shop floor or even by kitchen sink. Proper moral concern for the state of the population of Bangladesh is fine: sympathy with the chap on the 04.00 shift in a semi-derelict, unheated, dank, damp, draughty engine-shed: desperately trying to keep on the road, pieces of machinery for which maintenance funds are exhausted; and which have probably clocked up more than a million miles – that is not a group of people for whom middle-class mums would hold a fund-raising coffee-morning.

The truth is that many millions of people in Britain owe an untold debt, not only to the artisans and craftsmen who kept the locomotives going at the end of the steam era: but perhaps even more to the foremen and managers charged with the responsibility of keeping the trains on the move, and keeping the men at work. Just such a man was Ted Richardson. Born in the North-East, Ted epitomised all that is best about middle-management. In the private sector of industry he would have, and deserve, a senior position. On BR his talent, whilst acknowledged and undoubtedly appreciated, seemed not to have sufficient scope in

21

which to flourish, even as shedmaster at Feltham, where I came to know him well.

Finding one's way to Feltham shed for the first time was not easy. Returning to the site fifteen years after its closure was not any easier. Pictures tell a more eloquent tale, than words. (See page 28.) 'Twas ever thus. My catalogue tells me that my first visit to Feltham was on 11 May 1963: that day I photographed in colour, Drummond 'M7' 0–4–4T No. 30032: Maunsell 'Q' 0–6–0 No. 30548: Urie 'S15' Nos 30501/3: Maunsell 'W' 2–6–4T No. 31917: Urie 'H16' 4–6–2T Nos 30516/8/9 and Bulleid 'Q1' No. 33038. Herein lies the clue to Feltham's role, as the LSWR's main London-area freight shed and yard. Throughout its life, Feltham was a freight establishment. Never was she home for the glamorous express passenger locomotives. Perhaps that is why the place never drew much attention: perhaps that is why I found it such an attraction.

With the best will in the world, Feltham today is an unexciting place – and that is being diplomatic. The closure of the shed, the end of steam, the disuse of the large marshalling yard have removed perhaps its most important feature. Engulfed in London suburbia, it bears little resemblance to the small community mentioned in that most splendid book, Churton's *The Railroad*

PLATE 4. The LSWR built five 'H16' class 4–6–2Ts for short-distance freight work from Feltham. Classified '6F' by BR, they were unmistakable, and unusual in many ways. Note the splendid rivetting on the smoke-box of No. 30518

PLATE 5. The Boeing 707 coming in to land at Heathrow helps both to date and locate this photograph of 'Q' 0–6–0 No. 30548 on shed at Feltham on 11 May 1963. The last and perhaps the least successful of Maunsell's designs, not much improved by Bulleid's additions of multiple-jet blastpipe and large-diameter chimney. During the previous months, 30548 was on duty at Eastleigh as stand-by snow-plough engine, a duty no longer needed by the date of the photograph. (*opposite*)

Book of England. Indeed Churton himself in his introduction dated August 1851, writes in a style far removed from H. V. Morton. Of Feltham itself there is but one sentence:

> 'A retired spot, most pleasingly situated, and containing a few pretty villas, but nothing particular to notice.'

An updated Churton would be a fascinating book indeed.

My railway photography was usually unorthodox, in that I sought whenever possible to isolate myself from other enthusiasts, and especially other photographers. To do this meant forsaking the traditional locations, both line-side and shed scene. What was equally clear was that I obtained as much pleasure from photography of freight as of passenger trains and locomotives. And there was a particular challenge about shed photography, with endless vertical objects always seeming to stick out of the chimney.

As a commuter from Sunningdale to Waterloo, I passed Feltham ten times a week by rail. Always hopefully to be anticipated was the sight of an early morning west-bound inter-regional freight, steam-hauled, in a photogenic location. Depending obviously on variable factors, such as the time-keeping of the Sunningdale to Waterloo train on which I was travelling, the punctuality of the freight's departure from Feltham Yard, and the size, speed and motive-power of the freight-train itself, I could expect our paths to cross somewhere between Virginia Water and Staines, although not infrequently it was awaiting the exit road from Feltham Yard itself. During the period when my photography coincided with my commuting on this line, and up until the time of the diesel take-over of all SW Division freight, including Feltham, that train produced varied motive power.

The most usual locomotive was a Maunsell 'S15' 4–6–0 or a Bulleid 'Q1' 0–6–0: occasionally a Urie 'S15', Maunsell 'Q'; or rarely, a 'W' 2–6–4 tank: or a Bulleid Light Pacific.

Perhaps you can imagine my predicament in attempting to photograph the train. Staid commuters from Ascot, Sunningdale or Virginia Water initially looked askance at a chap with a camera entering the compartment. When it became clear that he intended to use it, feet shuffled, *Times* and *Financial Times* were carefully rearranged. The art of manoeuvering towards and opening the window, camera at the ready, on a wet or wintry day was not always accomplished with bonhomie.

The best location for the photograph was when the freight passed my e.m.u. on the sharp bend at the west end of Staines Central Station. The steam engine was accelerating away from the speed-restricted area of the station, as the e.m.u. was slowing down for the Staines stop.

PLATE 6. As a freight shed adjacent to a large marshalling-yard Feltham's motive power allocation included 'S15's for over 40 years. Both Urie and Maunsell types were based there. Reliable yet not glamorous, the 'S15' was at the heart of Southern Railway freight movements, within which Feltham played an important part. No. 30824, seen here simmering inside the depot on 16 May 1964, was one of the early Maunsell engines, introduced in 1927. She spent some years at Salisbury, was transferred to Feltham in December 1963, and surprisingly, to Basingstoke in June 1965 for the last 3 months of her life. Withdrawn in September that year 30824 returned to Feltham in store, and made the final journey to Cashmores, Newport, where she was cut up in December. Alongside is sister-engine number 30842, from the final Maunsell batch: both 'S15's were amongst the final five active survivors of the class. (As is clear, I did not possess a wide-angle lens.) (*previous pages.*)

PLATE 7. Another camera-shy class of Southern freight engine, was Maunsell's 'W' class 2–6–4 tank engines, whose appearance recalled their ill-fated indirect predecessors, the SECR 'River' class tanks. Like much else Maunsell built, they were handsome and reliable, and performed effectively on heavy short-haul freights around the London area. Just a few days prior to withdrawal, No. 31924 is seen here, on 3 July 1964, on shunting duty in Staines Central yard. (*opposite*)

Colour shots of Feltham freights on the electrified lines between the yard and Reading via Ascot, or the SW Main Line via Virginia Water and Byfleet Junction, are rare (see *In Search of Steam*, pages 30–31). They represented in their final years a lingering link with steam: an oasis of life in a sea of electrified lifelessness. As we sped past Feltham shed and yard my gaze was always aimed wistfully at the sight of wisps of steam in the vicinity. Steam declined and finally disappeared in 1967. Plans to build a diesel depot nearby, never materialised. The area of shed and yard is derelict, an ugly monument to the end of steam, made bitter by the wasted resource represented by the unused asset of the land.

Funny place, Feltham.

2 Castle's Checkmate

Like Collett's masterpiece, the castle on the chessboard does not need more than a single invitation to show his ability to move swiftly and directly to his destination. To suggest that the 'King' is slow and ponderous in comparison to the 'Castle' may be carrying the railway/chess analogy too far; yet few except those unwilling to acknowledge the supremacy of the GWR would deny that, all factors considered, the GWR 'Castle' Class 4–6–0 was the finest 'four-star' locomotive ever to run on Britain's railways. They were my favourite engine.

My pretensions to authorship preclude my attempting to write a definitive history of any particular class of locomotive, place, person or event of significance in the saga of Britain's railways. Not for me – or for you therefore, dear reader – the *Ibid*, the [22]*HLRO*, the *Infra*, or the *Op cit*: I have no ambition to acquire quotability, or wish to drive my readers to distraction by cross-references, visits to libraries or discussions with the bank-manager for the purpose of acquiring the necessary funds to purchase books referred to! In other words, so much has been documented about Collett's 'Castle' class engines that all I can offer is a personal testament from my memory and from my camera.

The first 'Castle' that I photographed in colour was neither a genuine Collett, nor even an authentic GWR locomotive. No. 7022 *Hereford Castle* was completed in June 1949, some eighteen months after the demise of God's Wonderful Railway. The date of my photograph was 26 January 1963, the location was the magnificent roundhouse of St Philips Marsh, Bristol. (See Plate 50.) The engine and its surroundings deserved each other: both have now gone. *Hereford Castle* ended her active days at Gloucester (Horton Road) MPD (85B). Withdrawn in June 1965, a mere stripling of sixteen years, she was cut down in her prime, and cut up at Birds of Bridgend that October. She had run 733,069 miles on active service.

Not until writing this chapter have I previously extracted from my photographic records a complete list of one specific class of locomotive that I photographed. Here is my 'Catalogue of Castles in Camera':

Number	Name	Date Built	Photograph Location	Date Photographed	Withdrawal	Mileage run (where known)
4079	Pendennis Castle	Feb. 1924	Swindon	26.7.63	June 1964	1,758,398
4082	Windsor Castle	April 1924	Old Oak Common MPD	5.7.64	Sept. 1964	—
4098	Kidwelly Castle	July 1926	Old Oak Common MPD	23.6.63	Dec. 1963	1,723,879
5000	Launceston Castle	Sept. 1926	Bristol Barrow Road MPD	28.6.64	Oct. 1964	—
5001	Llandovery Castle	Sept. 1926	Old Oak Common MPD	3.63	Feb. 1963	1,855,495
5014	Goodrich Castle	June 1932	Sonning Cutting	15.2.64	Feb. 1965	—
5018	St Mawes Castle	July 1932	Reading Sonning Cutting	4.5.63 2.11.63	Apr. 1964	1,503,642
5038	Morlais Castle	June 1935	Bristol: SPM and Temple Meads	26.1.63	Sept. 1963	1,438,862
5042	Winchester Castle	July 1935	Southall MPD	6.6.65	June 1965	1,339,221 (to July '64)
5057	Earl Waldegrave	June 1936	Old Oak Common MPD	23.6.63	Mar. 1964	1,273,324
5063	Earl Baldwin	June 1937	Oxford	11.5.63	Feb. 1965	—
5065	Newport Castle	July 1937	Old Oak Common MPD	3.63	Jan. 1963	1,222,961
5089	Westminster Abbey	Oct 1939	Bristol Barrow Road MPD	27.6.64	Nov. 1964	—
7000	Viscount Portal	May 1946	Didcot	4.5.63	Dec. 1963	824,873
7002	Devizes Castle	June 1946	Sonning Cutting	22.6.63	Mar. 1964	837,626
7004	Eastnor Castle	June 1946	Mainline, at Old Oak	3.63	Jan. 1964	876,349
7005	Sir Edward Elgar	June 1946	Sonning Cutting	22.6.63	Sept. 1964	869,370 (to end of '63)
7006	Lydford Castle	June 1946	Old Oak Common MPD	3.63	Dec. 1963	789,052

PLATE 8. Handsome is as handsome does: and a 'Castle' in Sonning Cutting on a fine summer day, was a jewel in a crown, albeit grubby by 22 June 1963, when I captured No. 7031 *Cromwell's Castle* speeding westwards with the 15.15 Paddington–Worcester express. In almost any weather Sonning presented the perfect backdrop for steam railway photography. No. 7031 was withdrawn a month later.

7018	Drysllwyn Castle	May 1949	Old Oak Common	3.63	Sept. 1963	614,259
7022	Hereford Castle	June 1949	St Philips Marsh MPD Old Oak Common MPD	26.1.63 23.1.65	June 1965	733,069 (to end of '63)
7023	Penrice Castle	June 1949	Near Twyford Sonning Cutting	29.6.63 15.2.64	Feb. 1965	—
7024	Powis Castle	June 1949	Bristol Barrow Road MPD and on mainline	27.6.64	Feb. 1965	—
7025	Sudeley Castle	Aug. 1949	Sonning Cutting	22.6.63	Sept. 1964	685,916 (to end of '63)
7029	Clun Castle	May 1950	Old Oak Common MPD ,, ,, ,,	23.6.63 5.7.64	Dec. 1965	618,073 (to end of '63)
7031	Cromwell's Castle	June 1950	Main Line Old Oak Sonning Cutting	3.63 22.6.63	July 1963	749,715
7032	Denbigh Castle	June 1950	Sonning Cutting	2.11.63	Sept. 1964	666,374 (to end of '63)
7034	Ince Castle	Aug. 1950	Weston-super-Mare	8.6.63	June 1965	616,584 (to end of '63)
7035	Ogmore Castle	Aug. 1950	Sonning Cutting	22.6.63	June 1964	580,346

To write a diatribe about each picture would doubtless bore to distraction. Nevertheless one cannot cease to be amazed at the interest in the *minutiae* of the details of the life and times of the 'Castle's, and indeed of most steam engines, particularly the named express locomotives. I shall mention later the Herculean task undertaken by P B Hands in compiling his series of booklets under the series title *What Happened to Steam*. In his introduction to Volume One he states 'All the information contained in this booklet has been compiled as accurately as possible, having taken seven years of intensive research concerning all the steam locomotives running on British Railways since January 1957 until their demise in August 1968.'

What a task! Yet there seems an almost insatiable demand for railway books about the steam age. If my records can help to fill any gaps in other enthusiasts' thirst for information – so much the better.

What can my list offer? How shall I select a few photographs on which to comment? One or two stand out. My photograph of 4079 *Pendennis Castle* at Swindon is of interest in that her decrepit external condition was soon to be transformed by

PLATE 9. Only a handful of GWR-built Castle's lasted into 1965. Of these No. 5042 *Winchester Castle* became the last survivor, being withdrawn in June. Note the flat-sided tender. Her final transfer was to Gloucester (Horton Road) MPD the previous July. When I saw and photographed her, at Southall Shed on 6 June, a few days before her withdrawal, she was a sorry sight indeed, with battered chimney, safety-valve cover missing and leaking steam everywhere. Her name and number-plates, smoke-box and shedplate have gone and '5042' is chalked on her buffer-beam. How are the mighty fallen. (*opposite*)

PLATE 10. Probably, and justifiably, more has been written about the 'Castle's than of any other class. Photographed at Old Oak Common MPD in March 1963, No. 5065 *Newport Castle* was already withdrawn. The class remained a standard type, with only detail alterations, for 38 years, and indeed was 'under construction' from 1923 until 1950: an astonishing record for an express passenger locomotive class. *Newport Castle* has lost her cabside number-plate, but smoke-box number is still intact. Ere long such trophies would become sought-after acquisitions, not to be left on withdrawn engines. Also in camera is 'King' Class 4–6–0 No. 6010 *King Charles I*, withdrawn from Cardiff Canton MPD the previous June, stored at Old Oak Common Works until November 1963, thereafter stored at Swindon Works until August 1965 and scrapped there that month. (*overleaf*)

restoration at the behest of Mr W. H. McAlpine. Her subsequent export to Australia pleased me not at all. I was at Avonmouth Docks the day she arrived for loading aboard the ship that would take this historic British locomotive across the world. Bill McAlpine doubtless did not share my views on his transaction, but this was the 'Castle' that, in 1925, went to King's Cross in the locomotive exchanges that year, and showed the LNER what a good engine could do on the East Coast Main Line. I shall continue to press Government to require a licence to be obtained for the export of significant pieces of our national railway history, even if they are less than fifty years old. After all, under present regulations any of the 1930s engines including *Mallard* could be sold to the highest bidder around the world.

Information about one's own photography emerges from preparing lists like that on pages 31/32. The realisation that one has photographed the same engine at different times in different locations is knowledge brought to one's attention only now, some eighteen years later in the case of the two listed shots of No. 5018 *St Mawes Castle*, in May and November 1963. Again, the call of steam dictates another minor memorial, to be remembered, recalled and savoured.

Perhaps the most fortunate photograph is the one of No. 5089

PLATE 11. A BR-built member of the class, No. 7031 *Cromwell's Castle* hastens the 08.48 Droitwich Spa to Paddington train past Old Oak Common on the final stage of its journey, on a bright March day in 1963. Note the mixed stock. This engine was withdrawn after a mere thirteen years service. Recalling BR's finances, one wonders at the 'judgement' that allowed the anti-steam propagandists to perpetrate such an appalling waste of modern, efficient motive-power. The line to Birmingham is visible on the right of the picture. (*opposite*)

Westminister Abbey at Bristol Barrow Road on 27 June 1964, for this was one of the 'Castle's rebuilt from a Churchward 'Star' Class 4–6–0, in October 1939. The 'Star' Class four-cylinder express passenger engines were well-named: one of the truly outstanding new designs of the GWR's great Locomotive Carriage & Wagon Superintendent, G. J. Churchward. Introduced in 1907, they were undoubtedly pre-eminent amongst Britain's express passenger locomotives of their time. Indeed, arguably until the appearance of Nigel Gresley's first Pacific from Doncaster Works for the Great Northern Railway in 1922, the 'Star's were the envy of most of Britain's railways: not that they would admit it, of course!

That great railway historian, O. S. Nock, known affectionately as 'Ossie' throughout the railway fraternity, has splendidly tabulated the history of the 'Star's, 'Castle's and 'King's from 1906 to 1965: inception to death. No more grisly and grotesque a death did my camera recall, than that of another great performer, No. 5042 *Winchester Castle*. Glad as I was to be privileged to see her at Southall on 6 June 1965, her condition that day has left its mark on my memory through all the intervening years. She was the last of the GWR-built members of the class to survive in active service, being withdrawn just a few days after I saw her. Whether my photographs of her at Southall were the last colour shots of her in steam I know not, but it seems most likely.

Even this limited 'photo-call' contains some interesting engines. Taking them in 'photo-chronological' order, 5065 *Newport Castle* was named after an 'Earl' class 4–4–0, when built in July 1937; she had had the name *Upton Castle* allocated. Similarly 5063 *Earl Baldwin* was originally to be designated *Thornbury Castle*. The latter name was in fact placed on 7027, one of the BR-built engines. No. 5057 *Earl Waldegrave* entered service with the title *Penrice Castle*. The change, in July 1937, was part of a general change of name of a number of the class. The name 'Penrice Castle' reappeared on 7023 in June 1949.

In 1940–41 the 'Castle' names of Nos. 5071–82 were replaced by those of aircraft which had become proud badges of courage, and indeed household words, during the Battle of Britain.

No. 7034 *Ince Castle* was one of the last four engines built, in August 1950. No. 7005 *Sir Edward Elgar* was *Lamphey Castle* until renamed in August 1957. No. 4082 *Windsor Castle* underwent a 'character change' in February 1952, when the number and nameplates were transferred to engine No. 7013, and the number and name of 7013 *Bristol Castle* were transferred to 4082. This was done in connection with the train arrangements for the funeral of King George VI. At that time, 4082 *Windsor Castle*, the appropriate engine to haul the cortège, was in

PLATE 12. In the dying months of steam operation on Brunel's magnificent Great Western main line, each signal-change was followed by an agonising but expectant vigil, for railway photographers by the lineside, in those days that seem now so long ago. In winter, lack of sun was sometimes adequately compensated for by bright light and magnificent smoke billowing out and hanging in the cold air. Just such a day was 15 February 1964. If I close my eyes I can still see 7023 *Penrice Castle* sweeping imperiously up the main line through Sonning Cutting with the 11.10 Worcester–Paddington express. (*opposite top*)

PLATE 13. Not quite Russian Roulette, but squatting low down to obtain a picture at this angle, of a fast-moving engine, was not recommended, and I over-balanced – backwards, fortunately – immediately after clicking the shutter on this one: No. 7004 *Eastnor Castle* rapidly gathering speed on the main line near Acton Wells Junction. The train was the 11.15 Paddington–Worcester and Hereford, and the date March 1963. This line was the last on which steam performed the regular express passenger services from Paddington, with the 'Castle's invariably in charge. *Eastnor Castle* was one of the final batch of GWR-built engines, emerging from Swindon Works in June 1946. She was fitted with a double chimney in February 1958, and withdrawn in January 1964. (*opposite bottom*)

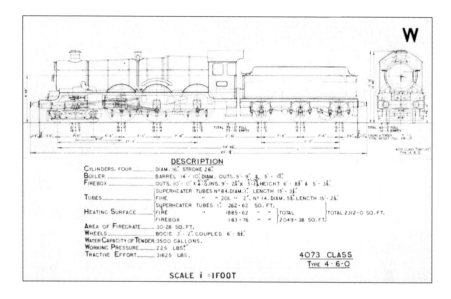

DESCRIPTION

CYLINDERS. FOUR ____ DIAM. 16." STROKE 26."
BOILER ____ BARREL 14'·10." DIAM. OUTS. 5'·9" & 5'·1½."
FIREBOX ____ OUTS. 10'·0" X 4'·5.INS. 9'·2¼"X 3·2½ HEIGHT 6'·8⅞" & 5'·3⅜."
TUBES ____ SUPERHEATER TUBES Nº 84. DIAM. 1." LENGTH 15'·3⅜"
FIRE " " 20L " 2". Nº 14. DIAM. 5⅛. LENGTH 15'·2⅝.
HEATING SURFACE ____ SUPERHEATER TUBES 1". 262·62 SQ. FT.
FIRE " 1885·62 " " TOTAL TOTAL 2312·0 SQ. FT.
FIREBOX 163·76 " " 2049·38 SQ. FT.
AREA OF FIREGRATE ____ 30·28 SQ. FT.
WHEELS ____ BOCIE 3'·2". COUPLED 6'·8⅞"
WATER CAPACITY OF TENDER. 3500 GALLONS.
WORKING PRESSURE ____ 225 LBS."
TRACTIVE EFFORT ____ 31625 LBS.

4073 CLASS
TYPE 4·6·O

SCALE ¼ =1 FOOT

MICROGRAPH I. As the first of BR's working drawings to appear in this book, I pay tribute and say 'thank you' to Bill Tasker, who keeps many thousands of technical drawings at Euston. As dedicated to his property as any top-link engine man to his steed, Bill gave unstintingly of time and advice as I browsed around his private world.

Surely no photograph can do more justice to the classic 'Castle' lines than this outline dimensional drawing. My preference for Collett's four-cylinder masterpiece above all other locomotives is confirmed by study of this extraction from Swindon.

For non-technical readers, the small front-end view (top right) shows what is meant by a 'four-cylinder locomotive'.

Swindon Works undergoing heavy repairs. She was the 'appropriate' engine because King George V had driven her himself during a visit to Swindon works on 28 April 1924. It was a rather poor show that the name and numberplates of 4082 and 7013 were never switched back: that would never have occurred in GWR days, I am certain.

Although my listed photographs include only twenty-eight different engines, there are some famous members of this class even by their own outstanding history: to mention but two, 4079 and 5000. The former as mentioned earlier, went to King's Cross in the 1925 exchange trials with the LNER, and thrashed that company's selected steed on her home ground. This famous occasion still fascinates enthusiasts, and breeds argument fed on loyalty and prejudice almost sixty years on. Indeed, an excellent 'apologia' for the LNER appeared in the December 1981 edition of *Railway World* by G J Hughes, under the title 'Not a fair trial?' Just as well there was a question mark! The following year, 5000 was put to work on the LMS West Coast Main Line – resulting in a request from LMS to GWR to build them fifty 'Castle's – an order declined by Swindon. (Although this request is denied by some my information came first hand from an impeccable source – the late K J Cook.)

Some of the mileages are unknown because records appear not to have been kept by London Midland Region after transfer of depots from Western to Midland regional control. Naturally, standards outwith the GWR were lower . . .

The withdrawal of 7029 *Clun Castle* saw the end of the four-cylinder locomotive in British Railways' ownership.

3 Rain, Steam and Speed

I do not know whether Turner was the first famous railway enthusiast, or even the first railway artist of renown. Certain it is that, over the years, artists and authors, poets and photographers of differing talents, have sought to capture for posterity the peculiar magic of the steam railway. Perhaps because the invention of the steam locomotive so utterly transformed man's existence: perhaps because it bred such a wealth of characters over so many years: perhaps ... perhaps .... Whatever the reason, that great gaunt metal machine evokes an affection rarely if ever bestowed by *homo sapiens* upon one of his own creations.

By overcoming the elements man, through steam, mastered his environment. The greater the challenge the more dramatic the achievement. That is why Shap was such a magnet. Indeed, Rain, Steam, and Speed, in its illustration of a great viaduct, added the element of civil engineering to the tribute paid by Turner to the drama of the scene he so superbly set out to portray.

Rain, Steam, Speed: you feel it, you see it, you smell it. Thus are the three senses aroused. Add to that the spice of a battle against the elements, and the dramatic apparition produced by Turner encapsulates the lure of steam. What Turner knew would appeal to his viewers seems to be borne out today, by the reaction to some of my murkier photographs. Whilst those without real commitment to railway enthusiasm eulogise shots of clean engines in the sunshine of Sonning Cutting, the hard-core enthusiasts specify preference for those photographs epitomising steam's struggle with the elements: indeed not just with the natural elements but with the neglect, disdain, even hatred of the steam-engine displayed by members of BR management in the 1960s. Thus the most appealing pictures turn out to be the most difficult to reproduce. Authors paying tribute to their publishers, or to the printer, may seem strange, and may be tempting providence, yet it was those dark shots of dirty locomotives, leaking steam at every joint, struggling for a foothold or emerging

from the gloom, that generated the 'that was how it really was, at the end' remarks, as nostalgia weaves its web around those who recall the dying years of steam.

Mathematically out of 365 days in Britain, photographic conditions are only occasionally ideal for colour photography. It was ever thus. At the time of my crusade to record the passing of the steam era, colour film was less sophisticated than it is today, and printing techniques equally so. Thus was I diffident to select for book-reproduction some of the shots that by Turner's criteria might be construed to be the most evocative. Yet in this category is a good percentage of my 'library'. Perhaps, incidentally, I should make it clear beyond peradventure that I do not see myself as a latter-day Turner! Not for me the presumption of artistic talent; merely the good fortune to practise a hobby enjoyed by many, allied to photographic opportunities sought by yet available to few.

Those murky days of winter when one stood, wrapped in duffle-coat, huddled against the cold, camera at the ready, seem an age away, an era gone. Be it remote rural sanctity, urban gloom or the peculiar magic of steam engine shed, I know that no other circumstance, no other creation than the steam locomotive at work, could draw me from the comfort, warmth and dryness of

PLATE 14. Rain, Steam and Speed. The original by Turner (*National Gallery*).

PLATE 15. Bank Hall MPD Liverpool seems to have escaped attention from railway photographers. On 4 July 1965, 'Jubilee' 4–6–0 No. 45684 *Jutland* emitted ample evidence of life and spirit, dappled by sunlight fighting its way through the grime-encrusted murk of ages. Extremes of light and dark made shed-photography more art than science. (*opposite*)

PLATE 16. Although delayed, BR/Std Class '5' 4–6–0 No. 73031 gets to grips with the 10.40 Bristol (Temple Meads) to Newcastle train on 26 January 1963. (*left*)

PLATE 17. I was on hand on 15 February 1964 to capture 'N' 2–6–0 No. 31873 emerge through the fog as she pulled away from Farnborough North Station with the 09.45 Reading to Redhill train. (*right*)

PLATE 18. 15 February 1964 was a gloomy day, as seemed always attendant on my visits to the SW mainline. Emerging from the mist, on the up slow line near Farnborough, is Bulleid Rebuilt 'West Country' Pacific No. 34039 *Boscastle*, in charge of the 08.37 Bournemouth West to Waterloo slow. (*below*)

the daily round. One has only to write the word 'diesel' to know that those lifeless boxes are not worth a single raindrop. Can you see Turner painting an HST or yet a Class '33'? Just a few days before writing these words I was filling my car with petrol at a garage on the Christchurch By-Pass. Soporific as I stood, pump in hand squirting the liquid into the side of the car, I glanced up as a train noisily rumbled past on the embankment across the fields. It was a 'Deltic' hauling a special from Bournemouth to Waterloo. Who cared? Who noticed? Excepting those involved with their special working, it was a matter of singular disinterest. Yet if that had been *Lord Nelson* on the embankment across the fields, that would have been noticed. . . .

Rain, Steam and Speed . . . appreciation is in the mind. This chapter then seeks merely to evoke memories of times past. Perhaps, too, it may provide time for our thoughts of and thanks to the unsung heroes on the footplate, who did their best with ill-serviced, poorly-maintained machines, at inhospitable hours, in foul weather to keep the railway going.

PLATE 19. LMS duet: Stanier '8F' 2–8–0 No. 48451 and '4F' 0–6–0 No. 44181, coupled together Light Engine, hasten past Dallam Sidings Box, Warrington on 2 December 1964. (*previous pages*)

PLATE 20. Rebuilt 'West Country' Pacific No. 34040 *Crewkerne* with a Waterloo–Bournemouth express on the down fast line between Fleet and Winchfield, on 25 June 1965. Completed in September 1946, *Crewkerne* was rebuilt in October 1960 and cut up at Cashmore's, Newport in 1968. (*above*)

4 A4 Swansong

I suppose I *had* to write this chapter: not because I greatly admired the aesthetics of Gresley's *pièce de resistance*, but because, sooner or later such a chapter becomes inevitable. Omission in a railway book would be tantamount to writing about French cookery without mentioning *coq au vin* (I do not much like *coq au vin*, really). Nevertheless, setting aside my predilection for Gresley's 'A3', one has to admit that the 'A4' was an impressive sight, as must have been a dinosaur.

To my mind streamlining was mere gimmickry on the steam locomotive. The sight of a long, sleek boiler, suitably adorned with appropriate extrusions, exemplifies the visual appeal. Indeed a short fat boiler can have charm. Imagine how a streamlined 'M7' would look: quite so! But I digress: this is to chronicle and record by word and colour photograph the passing from the working scene of Britain's most eulogised railway-engine: and you cannot *all* be wrong.

The scope for photographing 'A4's in colour, within the timescale of my own endeavours, was limited. Indeed my efforts bore fruit only thrice, and on each occasion were more by chance than foresight. At King's Cross Top Shed in March 1963, No. 60007 *Sir Nigel Gresley* was on shed, undergoing repairs. At Peterborough's New England MPD on 7 July 1963, I found two members of the class, No. 60017 *Silver Fox* and No. 60034 *Lord Farringdon*. *Silver Fox* still displayed her silver fox, and looked impressive as she moved about the shed yard. Whatever one's views of streamlining one could not deny that the 'A4' was an impressive locomotive and the dark green BR livery suited and dignified the class considerably more than azure blue.

My third meeting was on a sparkling sunny day, 5 August 1965, at St Margaret's MPD, Edinburgh. And Scotland is at the heart of this chapter. On shed that day was No. 60027 *Merlin*, as well as other, and to my eye more attractive and exciting LNER motive power. I photographed, in colour of course, 'V2' 2–6–2

Nos. 60955 and 60835: 'A3' Pacific No. 60041 *Salmon Trout*: 'B1' Nos. 61076 and 61396: and most interestingly, the shed's stationary boiler: 'J36' 0–6–0 No. 65234 became one of the oldest locomotives that I was fortunate enough to photograph between 1962–68. But I am sidetracking myself again: this chapter is supposed to be about the 'A4's. As I said, Scotland is at the heart of this chapter: and steam cognoscenti will indeed know why. For, of all the events that chronicled the decline and fall of steam, the saga of the introduction of the 'A4's, quite unexpectedly, on to the three-hour Glasgow–Aberdeen express service, in 1962 remains a memory that time and some fine photographers will never erase from the memory of a most melancholy era.

For years have I wondered about those 'A4's on the Glasgow–Aberdeen trains. How did they really perform? What did the men think of them? What condition were they in after more than 30 years hard graft? Lacking any of my own photographs of their final main-line fling, how could I justify including in this or any other book a chapter featuring the class? My decision was reached: I should revisit, not only the site of my last working 'A4' photography: but the site of their 'last stand'. Thus in October 1981 I set out for Edinburgh and Aberdeen. What a time I had!

This is my third railway book. In both *British Steam in Cameracolour* and *In Search of Steam* my confessions flowed. This book maintains that established tradition. The framework around which my visit to Scotland in October '81 was built, was twofold: to visit some of the more distant Holiday Inn hotels, and to attend the Conservative Party Conference in Blackpool. It is no part of this book, in spite of my self-created link with H. V. Morton, to write a gazeteer of Scotland or indeed of Blackpool. Of one it is impossible to have too much: of the other, too little. The one provides the reason, excuse, opportunity, to spend time *en route* to, and visiting, the other. In a sentence, Party Conference in Blackpool allows me to justify a bi-annual visit to Scotland with Jane: and as ever in my life one thing leads to another! Thus we arrived in Edinburgh on a sunny but cold day, Tuesday – 6 October 1981. My tasks were three: to attend a meeting with the Scottish Tourist Board; to inspect the site of a potential Edinburgh Holiday Inn; and to revisit Edinburgh St Margaret's MPD. We tackled these tasks in the reverse order to those outlined above.

Jane has grown wearily accustomed to a man whose railway enthusiasm and political activities have produced a distinctive style of lunacy. Over the years, she has become inured to searching for, and often finding, places to which normal mortals are rarely attracted. Thus that October morning, she was

PLATE 21. Having photographed No. 60007 *Sir Nigel Gresley* at King's Cross Top Shed in March 1963, I was fortunate to capture the same locomotive at Peterborough New England on 7 July 1963, during her brief residential sojourn there. Transferred to New England (34E) in June after many years based at King's Cross (34A), 60007 was soon on the move north again: in October '63 she moved home once more to St Margaret's, Edinburgh. Here she remained for nine months before her third move in just over a year, and this time her last in BR ownership – to Aberdeen Ferryhill (61B). Here she is in notably clean condition, and her white buffers indicate very recent special care and attention to appearance. (*previous pages*)

PLATE 22. My first photograph of a Gresley 'A4': and surely no more appropriate a member of the class was on hand to confront my Voigtlander's lens, than No. 60007 *Sir Nigel Gresley*, seen undergoing repairs in March 1963, at King's Cross Top Shed –itself the most celebrated haunt of the class. Now restored to main-line running, and in pristine condition. I feel obliged to state my preference for BR's green livery, as discernible here, to the rather vulgar blue in which this engine is now coated. For me, Gresley's 'A3' is to the 'A4' as is an athlete to an all-in wrestler, although perhaps the sight of 60007's smoke-box door in this photograph of an 'A4' with the lid up, is more akin to a peep behind a fat lady's blouse!

resigned, rather than surprised, to find herself twisting through the back-doubles of Edinburgh in search of an engine shed; as guide I consulted the self-same copy of the Ian Allan *Shed Guide* (Price 3/6) that I had used whilst conducting my frantic search for steam in the '60s.

Having extrapolated the 'walking instructions from Waverley Station' into the best way to reach St Margaret's by car, we found ourselves cruising slowly down London Road, looking for Clockmill Road.

'I don't remember that stadium', I mused. No comment. 'Or that office block. It's somewhere around here, though.' No comment. 'Stop darling, I'll ask that woman on the corner.' With muttered abuse about stupidity, driving difficulties and other totally deserved admonitions, we stopped. 'Excuse me ... can you tell me where Clockmill Road is?' Silence: quizzical look: pause for thought: glance at questioner to see if he is both sober and serious. 'Och, it must be a wee while since you were here.' Having confirmed the accuracy of her remark, I opined that indeed it was some sixteen years since my last visit to the immediate vicinity. On telling the good lady that I was searching for the old engine shed, she proffered the information that would have been mine had I been remotely interested in the

rationalisation of BR motive power depots since the end of steam.

St Margaret's shed had been demolished years ago. On and adjacent to the site, now stands, perhaps inevitably, a characterless pile, filled no doubt with hundreds of faceless bureaucrats: the sign at the entrance to the building said it all – Scottish Office. Employing the standard tactics of the experienced trespasser I persuaded Jane to drive unhesitatingly into the main entrance and head for the extremity of the car-park. Twisting and turning round the complex of buildings, we reached the end of the car park, right up against the fence alongside the main line into Waverley Station; a mere double track, without a single point. The historic significance of the site has been obliterated.

Parking the car, I started to search for some reminder of St Margaret's past, some totem, some memento. A small pile of sleepers alongside the fence was poor reward. The solitary reminder of times past, is the old stone wall that separates the site from London Road, on the escarpment high above. Notwithstanding the boring barren bleakness of the area formerly occupied by the depot – thoroughly typical of modern planning and construction – my mind drifted back to that sunny August day in 1965, when *Merlin* posed for me on the shed's turntable. I

Fig. 7. The shed is on both sides of the line about 1½ miles east of Waverley Station. The yard is visible from the line.

Turn right outside Edinburgh Waverley Station along Princes Street, continue along Waterloo Place, Regent Road, Montrose Terrace and London Road. Turn left into Clockmill Road and the shed entrance is on the right-hand side. Walking time 30 minutes.

This extract from the 1961 edition of *The British Locomotive Shed Directory* was my guide when searching for St Margaret's Shed. Clockmill Lane is now the only surviving thoroughfare in Edinburgh to bear the name once familiar to railwaymen and enthusiasts.

recalled, too, the antiquated coaling mechanism that lasted until St Margaret's steam demise: no trace remained in this infertile wilderness. Remembering another shot taken, almost where I stood, of *Merlin* alongside 'V2' No. 60835, I shuddered. For once, Jane's plea for an immediate departure was barely resisted, as my camera clicked merely to recall my return to the scene of one of the 'A4's last stamping-grounds.

And so to Aberdeen! Careful students of previous literary effort by this author, will have learned of his predilection for endeavouring to kill two birds with one stone. The need to visit the Holiday Inn Aberdeen Airport, and the desire to spend a few days in Scotland, coincided with my signature of contract to write this book, and my commencement of this chapter. Thus the threads of differing interest caused me to contact Bob Kennedy, journalist on the Aberdeen *Press & Journal*, book reviewer and of course railway enthusiast. We had arranged to meet at his office during the morning of Wednesday 7 October, and he had agreed to arrange for us both to visit Ferryhill depot. It was not a desire to see a diesel depot that attracted me there. It was to be an unforgettable day, not so much for what I saw, but for whom I met and what I heard.

The approach and entrance to Ferryhill, indeed its location, set it apart from most other engine sheds. It is situated in a clean, smart and desirable part of the prosperous city of Aberdeen. In anticipation of whom we might meet, it was mildly frustrating when Bob Kennedy was unable to find the place! My 1965 edition of *The British Locomotive Shed Directory* was of little use, because our approach by car bore no relationship to the directions, in the Directory, for walking to the shed from the station. Those directions themselves contain a poignant touch: 'The shed is on the west side of the main line just south of the Junction with the Ballater line.' The Ballater line no longer exists. However, just before mid-day we arrived, to receive a most friendly welcome from Charles Leaper, Area Train Crew Manager. In the next few hours I was to learn much about the 'A4' swansong on those Glasgow–Aberdeen three-hour trains in the '60s. But I was to be privileged to hear much else besides: how the feud between the North British and Caledonian Railways lives on today, almost sixty years since their independent demise. But that is another story perhaps; another chapter. I am searching for that chapter title as I write these words; no doubt it will come to me. Meanwhile, back to Ferryhill's role in the Swansong of the 'A4's.

The inexorable spread of the diesel meant that the days of express passenger steam were numbered by 1960. The arrival of the 'Deltic's on the LNER main lines, signalled the death-knell of the 'A4'. No. 60025 *Falcon* left Leeds Central on 15 June 1963

PLATE 23. The diagonal yellow stripe on the cabside denotes the impending end of steam. All engines thus branded were banned from operating on the electrified lines south of Crewe: an unlikely haunt for No. 60027 *Merlin* seen here on the turntable at her home shed, Edinburgh St Margaret's (64A) on 5 August 1965. Bright sun, deep shade and grimy locomotive made colour photography subject to errors of exposure and aperture. This site today is utterly transformed for the worse. (*previous page*)

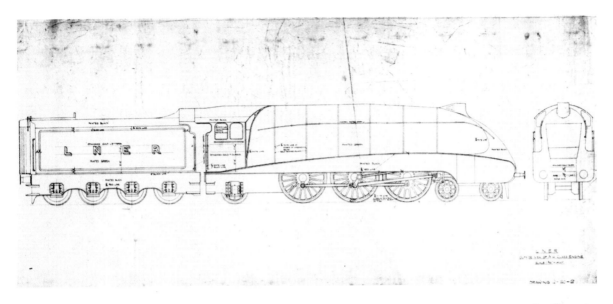

MICROGRAPH II. Comparison of this drawing of Gresley's 'A4' with the 'Castle' on page 38 surely justifies my preference for the Collett engine. I never could see the magic in the 'A4's: although credit is due to the LNER publicity machine for the public esteem in which the class was held. The removal of the skirting covering the motion and wheels helped – for my eyes – the appearance somewhat, diminishing the plastic-bag lines. Derek Cross has credited the 'A4's with the appearance of a pregnant whale. Whereas the front-end view of the 'Castle' on page 38 looks stylish and businesslike, the same angle here shows more of a hunchback than a thoroughbred.

with the very last steam-hauled 'White Rose' bound for King's Cross. Towards the end of 1963 the last 'A4's on the Eastern Region were transferred to Scotland, together with four from Gateshead. By this time the remaining members of the class, along with a few 'A3's held a virtual monopoly of the Glasgow (Buchanan Street) to Aberdeen expresses. Their introduction on to this route had little to do with romance, although sentiment and enthusiasm have over the years perhaps given the decision to put the 'A4's on to these trains an aura of mythology. The reason was more prosaic: the thoroughly inadequate and unreliable performance of the North British Type '2' Diesels, known to the men as the '6100' class. As *Railway Observer* reported in the March 1963 edition 'The Glasgow–Aberdeen trains have been mainly steam-worked, and the NB diesels have been largely retired to less exacting work'. Although perhaps even more boring and inadequate than most diesels, the Type '2's and their troubles vividly illustrate the disadvantages inherent in the dogmatic decision to scrap steam, regardless of the remaining useful life-span of thousands of locomotives. Quotation from *Railway Observer*, February 1964, underlines my point in prosaic language:

GLASGOW–PERTH–ABERDEEN. In the last week of November, steam power was very much in evidence on passenger as well as freight working. During three days of continuous observation and travel on the line, with the sole exception of the uprated D6123, no single example of a North British type diesel at work was noted. A number are now visible from the main line lying in St Rollox Works yard dump.

The Ferryhill and St Rollox 'A4's continue to perform consistently well on the three-hour Aberdeen–Glasgow services, although most are in poor external condition.

The factual details of the transfer of a batch of 'A4's to Ferryhill has doubtless been well catalogued. Reference to that splendid journal *Railway Observer* and to P B Hands excellent series *What Happened to Steam*, detailing the whereabouts and demise, by class, of Britain's steam stock during their last years of service, shows that fourteen 'A4's were transferred to Ferryhill MPD (61B) from June 1962. The engines concerned, with date of transfer, were as follows:

60004	*William Whitelaw*	June 1962	
60005	*Sir Charles Newton*	October 1963	
60006	*Sir Ralph Wedgwood*	May 1964	
60007	*Sir Nigel Gresley*	July 1964	Preserved
60009	*Union of South Africa*	June 1962	Preserved
60010	*Dominion of Canada*	October 1963	Preserved
60011	*Empire of India*	June 1962	
60012	*Commonwealth of Australia*	October 1963	
60016	*Silver King*	October 1963	
60019	*Bittern*	October 1963	Preserved
60023	*Golden Eagle*	June 1964	
60024	*Kingfisher*	June 1966	
60026	*Miles Beevor*	October 1964	
60034	*Lord Faringdon*	June 1964	

Some of these engines were not long on active service at Ferryhill. Most were stored there upon withdrawal. Four have been preserved and/or restored since withdrawal. No. 60009, now owned by John Cameron and based at Markinch, Fife, is fired and driven occasionally by Ferryhill men who had charge of her in the sixties. My visit then, on 7 October 1981 was not to check on well documented fact, but to try to unearth some unrecorded personal memories and anecdotes from within the confines of the 'A4's last working place.

Formalities completed, Charles Leaper introduced me to Jack Ralph, Acting Traction Inspector: Ian Souter, Area Maintenance Engineer, Aberdeen; and Andrew Dowie, Maintenance Assistant. Having quickly established that I was a genuine enthusiast and not a snooping politician, my questions began. Charles Leaper and Jack Ralph needed little memory-prodding. The arrival of 60004/11 in June 1962 was the first occasion any of the locomotives was actually allocated to Ferryhill. As the occasion was recalled, the anecdotes flowed: about the engines themselves; about some of the drivers and firemen; about the journeys on their three-hour expresses.

Charles Leaper first came to Ferryhill as a cleaner, in 1947. He had moved around the LNER/Eastern Region, and returned to Ferryhill in 1967 after spells at Knottingley, Leeds Holbeck, Newcastle, Cambridge and the 'other' Aberdeen depot, Kittybrewster. He had in fact been declared redundant as a fireman at Ferryhill on the demise of steam. His recollections of the reign of the 'A4's at Ferryhill, began with memories of lengthy walks along the line upon the failure of yet another NB Type '2' Diesel! He remembered the stationmaster at Perth, always a stickler for timing on the expresses. Stopwatch in hand, he fretted impatiently as the crews manoeuvered the Pacifics into the necessarily precise position at the Perth platform-end, to take water. A slight inaccuracy, under the station master's stare ensured a 'bloody soaking'. 'Your book would be banned if you recorded the language used by the "A4" crews at that water-column in Perth.' The route taken by the 'A4's on the Glasgow–Aberdeen train took them south out of Aberdeen 'on the Caley road, to Kinnaber Junction: thence via Forfar to Perth: that's the way the "A4"'s went' said Charles Leaper.

'The Kinnaber through line was shut to passenger traffic in '67' he added. At the mention of the word 'Caley', Jack Ralph visibly twitched. In his 36th year at Ferryhill – he joined the LNER there in 1945 – he was a Passed Fireman, and relief Driver, when the 'A4's were allocated to Ferryhill. Notwithstanding that it was 1981, some 36 years since the railways were nationalised and almost 60 years since the grouping. Jack Ralph was a North British man, and fiercely proud of it, too. Being totally matter-of-fact, Jack 'explained' to me that the 'A4's were naturally good engines, because the LNER was the inheritor of things North British, whilst the LMS took over from the Caley. As he put it to me, with a twinkle in his eye, 'the Caley man *thinks* their engines are the best; the NB man just tells the truth!' To him NB was 'the cream'; was, and still is. His memories of firing the 'A4's in the '60s were favourable. 'The "A1"'s and "A2"'s were bad fireman's locos: you had twice as much shovelling as an "A4" – they were lovely smooth locos.'

Jack told me only to expect the truth about engines, from an 'NB' man! 'Those Caley men are biased: one once told me a "Black 5" was a good loco!'

During that day I came to know Jack Ralph well. We went off in the evening for a drink, and he told me some yarns about the old railwaymen. What fabulous characters they were. Perhaps my romantic soul causes me to see Scots and Scotland through rose-coloured spectacles; yet truly I find it harder to leave Scotland every time I go there.

By this time, we had been joined by Ian Souter and Andrew

Dowie. Ian had drawn me a splendid map locating Kinnaber Junction, and we had settled into a session of reminiscence and banter *par excellence*. We turned to talking of other characters, and Andrew Dowie suggested I should meet Gordon Tulloch, the oldest man on the shed, due to retire the very next Monday. He was due on duty at 1.10 p.m. As I waited to meet this next actor at the Ferryhill Theatre, Andrew Dowie told me of his involvement with the 'A4' Swansong. He had been Senior Shift Maintenance Foreman at Edinburgh Haymarket in the early '60s when the diesel depot there was being established. The 'A4's allocated to Haymarket at that time were farmed out to St Margaret's or Thornton for their maintenance, although they were still doing rostered turns from Haymarket, and doing 30/35,000 miles between examinations. The conversation had switched to Edinburgh when I had asked what *Merlin* was doing when I photographed her at St Margaret's (see Plate 24) in August 1965. Mention of Haymarket shed produced another tale.

It seems that Haymarket in the 1950s was one of the last sheds to allow continuity of the practice of train-crews having their 'own' engines. Apparently some of the top link crews there bitterly resented the BR change to 'common-user' engines. On one occasion a crew from Haymarket ran to Dundee, only to find another crew rostered for their engine. They refused to quit their footplate, and frantic phone-calls ensued.

It was 1.10. There was a knock at the door, which opened to reveal a memorable face. Gordon Tulloch has very bright eyes, a ruddy complexion, shiny pate and an aura of experience. I knew we were in the presence of a Railwayman with a capital R. At Ferryhill for 45 years, he had been at Ballater prior to coming to Aberdeen. He told of the arrival of the Gresley 'P2's at Ferryhill. I would barely recall anything about 'P2's 'We got those Mikado's new: six of them were built for the Edinburgh–Aberdeen run. I remember 2002 – *Earl Marischal* I believe; and 2006 – was that *Thane of Fife*? ('P2' 2–8–2 No. 2006 was named *Wolf of Badenoch*: No. 2005 was *Thane of Fife*.) You remember – they were rebuilt to ''A2/2''s' he mused. 'I've seen them haul seventeen bogies without difficulty, on the 6.00 a.m. and 9.00 a.m. Passenger to Edinburgh.'

I turned his thoughts towards the 'A4's at Ferryhill in the '60s. He was well into the senior links at Ferryhill even then. 'They were pretty well gone by the time they came here.' Quietly, without seeking to make any dramatic points, he said there was 'nothing special' about driving an 'A4'. 'They were most awkward for disposal: and the sand-boxes were awkward, too. They were not really suitable for the Glasgow road – the ''V2'' was better. The ''A4''s did not have the adhesion on the hills.

They were all right south of Edinburgh. The management
thought they could do the 3-hour trains in the light of the failure
of the NB Type "2"s. But they were not ideal.' Gordon Tulloch
frequently worked the trains, and I doubt if a more authoritative
opinion, from the footplate, is available. If some of the Top Link
men driving and firing the 'A4's had reservations about their
suitability for the Aberdeen–Glasgow route, there was no lack of
enthusiasm amongst the Ferryhill maintenance staff, for whom
work on the class gave immense satisfaction and pride. To quote
Andrew Dowie 'To run out an "A4" on a trial run after renewal of
axleboxes was a marvellous thrill, and something happened to a
man in that he always took a lot of pride when he was next
allocated work on this class of loco.'

Digressing he chuckled as he told us the tale he had heard from
another driver, long since retired, of the stormy winter's night
when they came to a stand on the single-track section between
Montrose and Usan, with the 8.35 Sleeper. Sir Robert Boothby
was on board. As the driver tramped back to tell the guard,
Boothby stuck his head out of the window. 'What the hell's going
on?'

'We've run out of sand' said the driver, one Andy Gray. 'What
the hell have you got up there man, an engine or a camel!'

As an ill-informed Southerner I knew nothing of the saga of the
NB/Caley proposals to build a joint line; the feuds; and the
resultant single-track section. Our nation's railway history is so
rich, and men like Gordon Tulloch a proud legacy of that history.
When, suddenly, Charles Leaper invited me to present Gordon

Tulloch, there and then, with his long-service award. I did so with enormous pleasure. What a privilege.

That day seems endless! Ian Souter suggested I speak to Duncan Burton, now depot engineer at Haymarket, and a man reputed to be a wizard at setting the valves on Gresley engines. Jack Ralph said that Burton would set the valves just by listening to them. 'He got the drivers to run past the shed here at 25 per cent cut-off; he could tell which one was out. Setting valves on a Gresley engine was more an art than a science.' Jack told me about Eddie Parry – 'a Caley driver with a grudge against the ''A4''s. He was always grumbling about the sand not flowing.'

I must end this chapter – now! As I said at the start it is not intended to be an historic treatise. Indeed the 'A4's, in appearance, still leave me unexcited. Without their undoubted appeal however, I should never have contemplated this chapter; never visited Ferryhill; never presented an award to Gordon Tulloch; and never met Jack Ralph, his 'Bubbly Lamp' and his wonderful tales of Scottish enginemen. I might never have realised the significance of places like Kinnaber Junction – a ghost junction, now. That then will be the title for the next chapter – 'The Ghosts of Kinnaber'.

PLATE 25. In June 1963 the swansong of the 'A4's was presaged by their removal from King's Cross MPD: those that were not withdrawn forthwith were allocated to Peterborough New England (34E). My visit there on 7 July revealed 60007/17/34 on shed that day. The last of the class to enter service No. 60034 *Lord Faringdon* was about to take water when photographed. Originally named *Peregrine*, 60034 was renamed in March 1948, assuming the name of the last Chairman of the Great Central Railway who became one of the original directors of the LNER in 1923. He had been 'immortalised' on 'B3' No. 1394 which was scrapped in December 1947; thus the name Lord Faringdon lay fallow until taken by 60034.

5 Ghosts of Kinnaber

Of pride and prejudice there is plenty, on the old battlegrounds of north-east Scotland. What less would one expect from the descendants of the independent railwaymen of a proud nation? Of all the famous feuds that moulded the shape of our railways, none was conducted with keener rivalry and fiercer feeling than the battle between the North British Railway and the Caledonian Railway. The Race to the North, to Aberdeen in 1895 between these two was a race to reach Kinnaber Junction, the point at which each Company's lines converged for the final few miles to Aberdeen over shared track. To imagine that the rivalry ceased at the 1923 Grouping, is totally to misunderstand not only the nature of the Scots but the breed of 'homo sapiens' called 'railwaymen'. Further to presume that nationalisation in 1948, followed by the years of Beeching and diesel, has eroded the memory of fierce pride and competition that characterised the Scottish railway scene of yore, is again to err.

Under the Grouping, the Caledonian, together with the Highland Railway and the Glasgow & South-Western came within the ambit of the LMS: whilst the LNER incorporated the North British and the Great North of Scotland Railway. Thus the NB *v* Caley merely became LNER *v* LMS. Midnight on 31 December 1922 may have been the precursor of changed livery: but paint did not reach the hearts of the railwaymen. For the men joining LMS or LNER in the nineteen thirties at Aberdeen's Ferryhill or Kittybrewster sheds, names like London Midland and Scottish or London and North Eastern were distant and alien. Many of those men are now approaching retirement. Some are still based at Ferryhill. One of them is Jack Ralph, whose name I mentioned in the previous chapter. If 'JR' (the Dallas breed) is representative of Texans, then I'm glad I'm British. The 'JR' from Ferryhill is bred from strong stock. To share his heritage would cause me pride: to share his memories was my privilege and pleasure. The tales he told, and the manner of their telling, merely

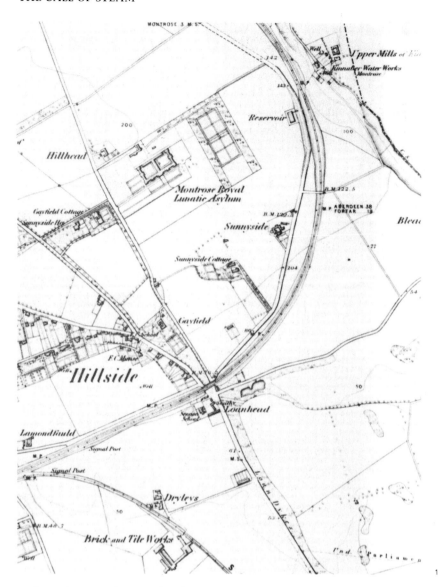

Fig. 8 (page 62) Fig. 9 (page 63) Fig. 10 (page 64) Fig. 11 (page 65)
Kinnaber Junction. In this series we trace the emergence of one of Britain's most famous railway junctions, and its subsequent decline. Map no. 1, dated 1862, marks the Upper Mills of Kinnaber and Kinnaber Water Works, alongside the railway line. By 1902, on map no. 2, Kinnaber Junction is marked in its own right (top centre). In 1923 (map no. 3), the Junction is a settled part of the landscape. By 1976 (map no. 4), we see signs of decline clearly visible to the discerning eye. The latest development – the end of Kinnaber as an operational BR junction – is not yet mapped.

1

reflect the sea-change that has come with the end of steam. To say that today's footplateman reflects his steed, means naught to those who have never met the 'men of steam'. Whereas modern locomotive performance is attributable to and affected only by the design of the unit, with a steam-engine it was the man who determined the performance. The spur of competition; the pride of 'the company'; the reward of skill and stamina used willingly to achieve a fine performance, all combined to create an elite band of men whose deeds live on in the memories of that dwindling corps of railwaymen, like Jack Ralph: Jack and his 'Bubbly Lamp', his 'Pourie' and his wit, the natural wit of a raconteur, a railwayman and a Scot.

Jack joined the LNER in 1945 and worked his way up the

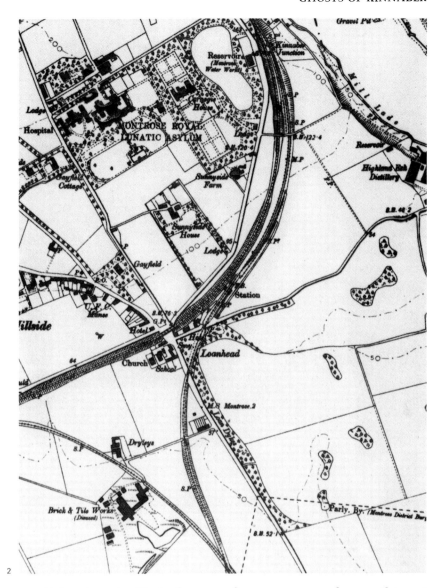

2

traditional route. He had a yarn for everyone and everything. I remember his description of firing a 'B1'. 'It was murder – they'd kick like a mule. It was like a 60-mile long staircase from here to Dundee.' Between Aberdeen and Dundee lies Kinnaber Junction, focal point of the Caley/NB feud. As the 'A4's flew the flag for Sir Nigel Gresley for the last time, it seemed that the Caley had won the final round, as the Glasgow-bound expresses took the Strathmore line from Kinnaber, by Forfar, Coupar Angus and Stanley Junction to Perth. Yet it was not to be. Precisely one hundred years from the Caley takeover, in 1866, of the Scottish North Eastern Railway, to give it a through route from Carlisle to Aberdeen, the 'A4's steamed into history. On 14 September 1966 No. 60024 *Kingfisher* ended an era as she swept through Kinnaber

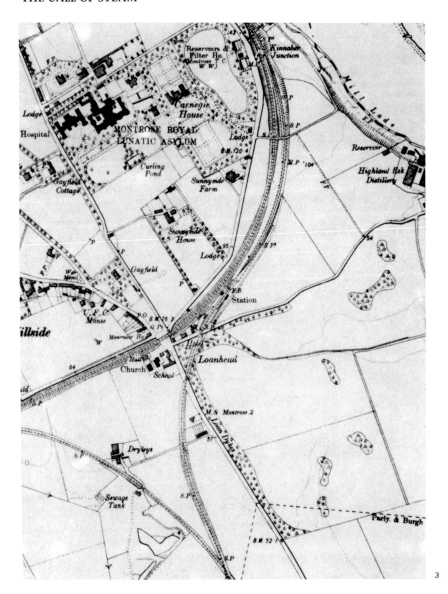

3

with the 08.25 Glasgow–Aberdeen. Within a year, the last passenger train had traversed the Strathmore line. On Monday 4 September 1967 most of the signal-boxes between Stanley and Kinnaber Junctions were closed. The line from Kinnaber to Bridge of Dun was singled and survived only to give freight access to Brechin. Kinnaber Junction, scene of drama and intrigue, survived as but a mockery of its own significance, until 1981. Now it has been totally eradicated as an operational BR junction.

I have to tell you that I had never been to Kinnaber Junction: had never heard of it before my day at Aberdeen Ferryhill in October 1980. But have you heard of Hurricane Hutch? Or

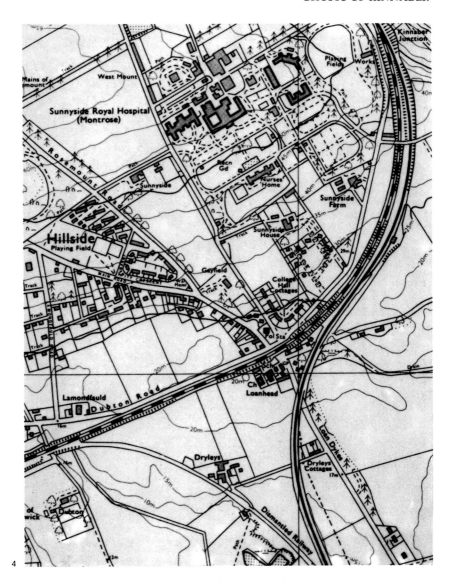

4

Spindles Murdoch? How about The Count: The Pimp: Smokey Joe: or Jock Henderson? These are the men of the Ferryhill Folklore: men of the great age of steam; of the rivalries between NB and Caley: the Ghosts of Kinnaber.

Like Jack Ralph, Jock Henderson was never parted from his Bubbly Lamp (to be pronounced Bobbly Lomp). He took not too well to transition from steam to diesel, refusing to be parted from his Bubbly Lamp whilst on diesel training. Entering a diesel engine-room, Jock's concession to flammability was to extinguish his fag, not his lamp!

Smokey Joe – Joe Mackintosh – was an LNER man, whose nickname derived from his complexion. He looked Spanish, but with his gutteral accent was as Scots as can be. His pipe, not his

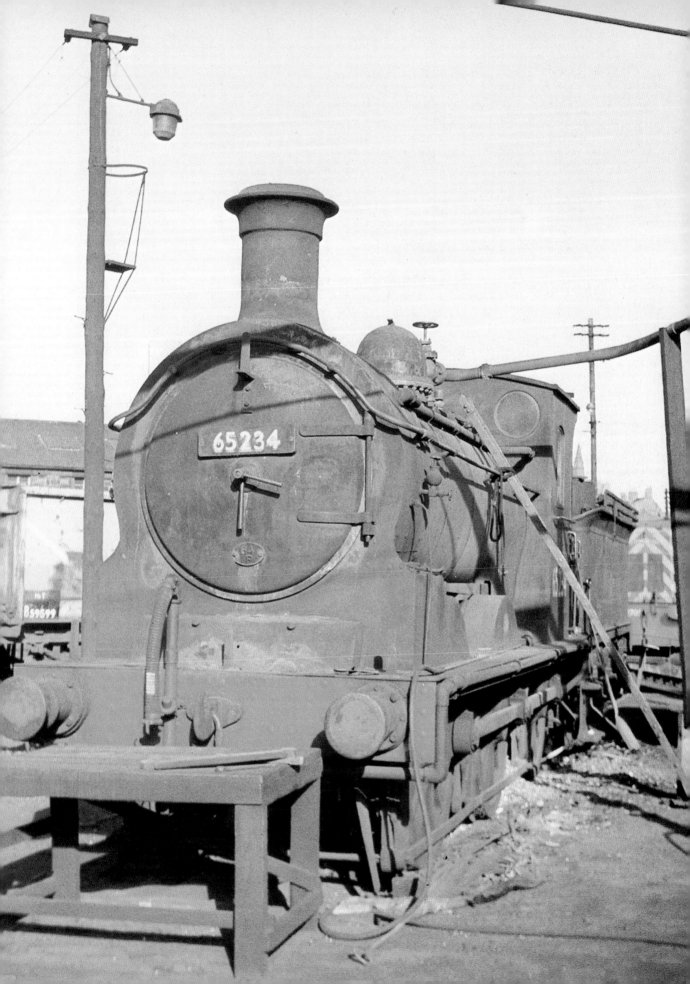

PLATE 26. Ghosts of the North British Railway echo around a locomotive belonging to a class introduced in 1888. Although immobile, former NB class 'C' (LNER class 'J36') 0–6–0 No. 65234 serves out her time as stationary boiler at Edinburgh St Margaret's on 5 August 1965. Not even the ladder leaning against her boiler, the missing dome cover or the stationary boiler attachments detract from the dignity of a 77 year-old veteran, who still retains both number and shed plate. Twenty-five of the class received appropriate names to commemorate service in France during World War 1. An odd event occurred to No. 65311 of the class. The name 'Haig' was unofficially painted on during summer 1953, and it remained thus for two years, when the engine entered Inverurie Works for overhaul. Very surprisingly 65311 emerged overhauled with name officially attached, and carried it until withdrawal.

lamp, was his soul-mate, attendance to which was, quite properly, a high priority. Stationed at Kittybrewster, he was working to Fraserburgh on one occasion when coupling-up the train seemed to be taking an inordinate time, causing his driver to come back to find out the reason for the delay. Smokey Joe was having trouble with his pipe . . .

Then there was 'Spindles' Murdoch: he was an LMS man. Coming off duty at Aberdeen Station, enginemen were frequently offered a 'lift' back to Ferryhill MPD on a light engine. Spindles was consistent: he would not ride the footplate of an LNER engine. 'The men aren't too bad – but I'd not trust myself on an NB loco.'

As Jack Ralph's memories unfolded, the anecdotes flowed. My enjoyment of the drams of Old Fettercairn Malt, increased as each character was revealed. Furiously I scribbled. Tales of their exploits, enthusiasms, misdeeds, seemed endless. 'I'll tell you about Hurricane Hutch' said Jack. Firing on a Black Five, they hit a farm tractor and cart loaded with neaps at an unguarded crossing. Believing attack to be the best form of defence, Hurricane Hutch berated the tractor-driver for his carelessness in being there. 'You nae goin' to say nothin' about it!' was the proferred advice.

I have had to delete two lurid tales about Hurricane Hutch; even though they are twenty years old my 'informant' fears the repercussions, even now! Pity, they were splendid tales, springing from Hurricane Hutch's enthusiasm. Yet he was not unique. For sheer bravado, Davy Tasker had a reputation for trying to 'knock the lum off' (lum = chimney). Legend at Ferryhill has it that some of the coal that Davy blasted up the chimney years ago is still in orbit.

Then there was 'The Count', whose real name I have been given, but had better not reveal, although like other footplatemen mentioned, their characters make them heroes not villains in my book! The Count was transferred from Kittybrewster MPD to Fraserburgh. Accustomed to regaling the opposite sex with his aristocratic lineage, he always wore a jacket and tie when driving, whatever the weather or circumstances. In the less sophisticated social scene in Fraserburgh compared to Aberdeen, he added to his sartorial elegance by the acquisition of a coat with velvet collar: apparently with results to justify the expenditure.

Jack's final character, the man whom he described as 'the greatest of the lot', was 'The Pimp'. Again, prudence dictates withholding his actual identity! Notwithstanding a deep, authoritative voice, The Pimp was constantly charged with breaches of discipline. His defence was invariable, positive and consistent. Always quoting Rule 127, 'The Driver must . . .'. The

PLATE 27. Few photographs taken as were mine between 1962–68 can satisfactorily portray the Ghosts of Kinnaber, other than to kindle the spirit of the pre-nationalisation railway. An LNER atmosphere pervades this scene of St Margaret's Shed, Edinburgh, with 'B1' 4–6–0 No. 61076 and 'A4' 4–6–2 No. 60027 *Merlin* prominent. Visible also is the smoke-box of BR/Standard 2–6–4T No. 80114. No doubt NB men would rejoice at the proper absence of Caley motive power! Note the 'B1's burnt smoke-box door, and the cabside yellow stripe on *Merlin*, whose tender appeared to be one of those fitted with corridor for dual-crew non-stop King's Cross–Edinburgh runs. (*previous pages*)

PLATE 28. Even the North British diehards at Aberdeen Ferryhill shed seemed not to have appreciated this ancient relic still amongst them, on the depot's Mess and Tool van. It was due to be scrapped just three weeks after this photograph was taken in October 1980. Perhaps it was appropriate that an NB, rather than a Caley relic, survived for so long after the demise of the A4s, the Strathmore line and the romance of the 'Race to the North'.

Pimp insisted his actions had been taken in compliance with his selected section of 127. On one occasion he was criticised by an Inspector of 'that other railway'. He told the Inspector where to go, with appropriate comments on both his parental and railway-operational heritage! Naturally by the time he returned to his shed, he was sent for by the shedmaster, and asked to apologise to the Inspector the following day. The next morning The Pimp saw the Inspector and beckoned him to his footplate: 'You don't have to go now', said the Pimp!

The Pimp's distinctive outlook on life was not restricted to railway matters. History was his speciality. 'The Middle East', he said 'was a peaceable place until British troops landed in Mesopotamia.' It seems that said troops, doubtless encouraged by The Pimp, took the labels of Nestlé's Condensed Milk tins and advised the locals that they were British Government cheques! As The Pimp said, 'When the locals went to the British Embassy to redeem their "cheques" they were thrown out, and there has been nothing but trouble since.'

Such are some of Jack Ralph's anecdotes. True or imagined, in substance or detail – who knows? Of one thing you can be sure: the steam age bred great characters, with hearts as big as the boilers on their engines. Most have gone: of them, their memories, their steeds, their railways, we have too little left behind. Walking the weed-strewn, disused lines, seeking the sites of dismantled stations, signal boxes, junctions, we can only dream of a proud, exciting vivid past . . . dream of the ghosts, of men, of machines . . . the ghosts of Kinnaber, as Caley & NB raced for the North . . . we shall never see those stirring times again.

6   M7

I was in my early thirties when first I photographed an 'M7', in February 1963. Introduced at the end of the last century, these locomotives were a lasting tribute to the quality of Victorian engineering: not to mention their being a living tribute to Dugald Drummond. Whilst the sophisticated public-relations activities of the LMS and LNER ensured a wide public knowledge of the names Stanier and Gresley, the Chief Mechanical Engineers of an earlier era were often unknown outside the railway world. Only now, in retrospect, is due attention being paid by a wider audience to the work of men of the pre-grouping companies: men like Dugald Drummond of the LSWR, to whose 'M7' 0–4–4 tank-engines this chapter is dedicated.

The 'M7' was the first new locomotive of Drummond's design, to emerge from Nine Elms Works, in March 1897. The 0–4–4T wheel-arrangement had a decidedly Victorian air about it. Yet as late as 1932, after Stanier's arrival on the LMS, ten 0–4–4T locomotives were introduced, as a new class. Although often attributed to Stanier these engines were in fact designed by E. J. H. Lemon, acting Chief Mechanical Engineer (CME) of the LMS pending Stanier's appointment. Nevertheless it was some 35 years after Drummond introduced the 'M7', that these LMS engines appeared: they had all gone before the last 'M7' was withdrawn.

Drummond, and his South Western successor Robert Wallace Urie were both Caledonian men. Both brought many of the habits and design criteria of St Rollox, to Nine Elms. Left-hand drive became the new rule. Indeed Scottish robustness became a feature of SW motive power. At a glance, the 'M7' – one of Drummond's two new SW designs, both of which entered service on 1 March 1897 – could have been a Caledonian, North British or Highland Railway machine. One distinctive feature of the class was the flared chimney, owing nothing either to Scottish or SW tradition. On their introduction they became the largest and most

powerful 0–4–4 tank-engines ever built: their weight in working order, when new, was 60 tons 3 cwt. They had 5 ft 7 in. driving wheels, $18\frac{1}{2}$ in. $\times$ 26 in. cylinders, and the original 150 lb boiler pressure was soon raised to 175 lbs.

Drummond was the first man to hold the title of Chief Mechanical Engineer on the LSWR. Able yet obstinate, he is well described by Hamilton Ellis in his book, *The South Western Railway*: one of the first railway books I bought, price 30 shillings – after my 'rebirth' as a railway enthusiast.

Little modified between the Premierships of Lord Salisbury and Harold Wilson – for that was their life-span – Drummond's 'M7's were ultimately extinguished by lack of work, not lack of heart. Many of the 105 locomotives of the class built between 1897 and 1911 ran for more than $1\frac{3}{4}$ million miles in revenue-earning service, much of which service, certainly in their latter years, was completed on short-distance empty carriage stock (e.c.s.) work, carriage shunting and short branch-line work. It was not ever thus.

When the first 'M7' appeared, they quickly found favour throughout the LSWR system. Indeed in their earliest days they were put to work on the main line between Exeter and Plymouth, although a derailment at Tavistock on 6 March 1898 resulted in

PLATE 29. Like anyone born in May 1897 'M7' 0–4–4T No. 30249 had been to many places, seen many changes and was living a less hectic life by February 1963, when I saw her standing in Vauxhall Station. Note the dome top safety valves. Not many colour photographs of 'M7's at work exist so it is for historic interest rather than technical excellence that I have included this shot. In 1942, when enemy action put electric services on the Waterloo–Alton line out of action, 249 was one of the 'M7's that took over. At withdrawal, five months after this photograph was taken, she was the oldest survivor of the class. Note lamp brackets on bunker, above the duty-discs.

their being taken off these express turns. It was on the London suburban services however that the 'M7's did much of their finest work. Until 1915 they worked most of the suburban services from Waterloo, including many of the fast outer suburban trains. Their acceleration was a vital factor in maintaining the tight timetables. The class also worked some of the semi-fasts on the Alton and Portsmouth lines.

Many members of the class continued to work local passenger and branch-line trains for 60 years. They saw out the LSWR, then the SR: and so, on into BR after Nationalisation, by which time they had strayed far from their native LSWR tracks. I remember fondly the sight of those elderly Victorian masterpieces running into Three Bridges with the East Grinstead branch trains. I photographed 30055 approaching East Grinstead with the 13.08 from Three Bridges on 23 March 1963. Exmouth Junction had a big allocation of 'M7's to work the Devon branch-lines. One of the last depot's to operate the class was Bournemouth, where they were the mainstay of the service to Brockenhurst via Ringwood. Yet for memories of the 'M7's final years one needed to travel no further than the scene of their finest years — Waterloo.

Into the 'sixties — nineteen sixties! — a number of the survivors, based at Nine Elms, handled e.c.s. workings from Waterloo to Clapham carriage sidings. This was not easy work: the trains were heavy, and the timings tight, crammed in as they often were, amongst electric trains in profusion, as well as the remaining main-line steam. With 19,750 lb tractive effort some of the e.c.s. trains were a hefty challenge for a four-coupled tank, let alone locomotives over 50 years of age.

I write this as my train from Weymouth passes through Vauxhall Station: it is nearly nineteen years since my camera first alighted on an 'M7' simmering quietly in Platform 1, with her train of milk tanks. The station remains, but not the network of pipes used in connection with the milk traffic, now like the 'M7's merely a memory. Yet memories of ancient tank-engines like 30249, then in her sixty-sixth year, remain for me more vivid, somehow, than the great passenger express locomotives thundering along a main line. Together with the 'T9's, the famous Greyhounds, the 'M7' was Drummond's finest locomotive: indeed they were amongst the best tank-engines ever to run on Britain's railways, yet they never seem, even in this nostalgic age, to have attracted much attention. After nationalisation their looks were enhanced by the Eastleigh paintshop which turned them out in lined black livery. In spite of their longevity, the class retained their 'Drummond' shape throughout their lives. On 18 May 1963, *Flying Scotsman* was on shed at Eastleigh. I

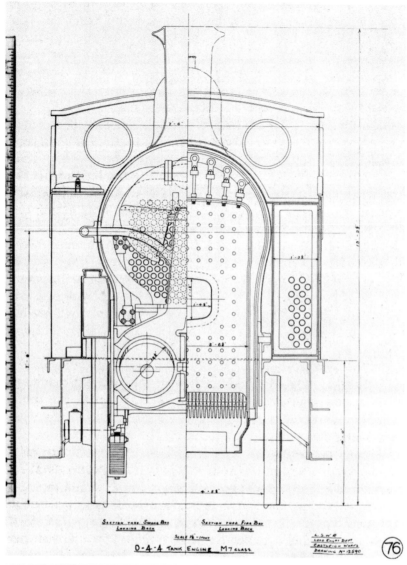

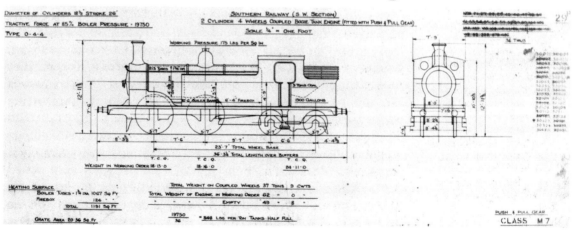

MICROGRAPH III. Even the hand-written notes on these drawings tell a fascinating tale. The side-view (below) of the 'M7' postdates the cross-sectioned view by some years. Indeed the former, although headed SOUTHERN RAILWAY (S.W. SECTION) has obviously been in use since the BR numbering scheme was introduced, in 1948, as can be seen by the hand-written BR numbers listed on the extreme right, whilst the SR numbers, top right, have been scratched out.

The sectioned view is superb. On the left-hand side is 'Section thro. Smoke Box Looking Back'. On the right-hand side is 'Section thro. Fire Box Looking Back'. The hand-written note at bottom right is most evocative. In addition to the interest in the technical detail, the Drummond chimney is shown to good effect, with its distinctive and delightful shape.

PLATE 30. On 11 May 1963, No. 30032 was on shed at Feltham. Built in March 1898, this engine went new to Bournemouth shed, and amongst other duties worked semi-fast services Bournemouth–Weymouth. Changes over the years included installation of LSWR cable and pulling gear for working push-and-pull trains, just prior to World War I. By the end of 1931 No. 32 was stationed at Nine Elms, working empty stock between Waterloo and Clapham, or carriage piloting at Clapham Junction sidings. She survived until July 1963, over sixty-five years of age. Evidence of the bulbous smoke-box door once a feature of the 'M7', is clearly visible. The Salter valves on the dome are also nicely visible

photographed the Gresley engine with 'M7' No. 30251 in the background.

Early on, thirty-one of the class were equipped with cable-operated push and pull gear in LSWR days: then in 1930 the SR converted all but one of these to the more reliable compressed-air system with the distinctive Westinghouse pump. Some of the class had their sandboxes on top of the leading splashers, with wingplates and a short frame overhang in front of the smoke-box. Thanks to the dedicated work of Bill Tasker in BR's archives department, I can illustrate how the 'M7' looked from the designer's viewpoint.

It is a sight that shall not fade from memory. 1964 saw the end of the 'M7' 0–4–4T. Gradually they were relieved of their remaining duties. By the beginning of the year, the survivors were not in good condition, often losing time or even becoming failures, due to lack of maintainence rather than heart. The Three Bridges engines were transferred to Bournemouth, and their last regular passenger duties were on the Swanage and Lymington branches. If only, if only . . .

The last on active duty was 30053, hauling a rail tour on 5 July 1964, although officially withdrawn, along with her remaining eight sisters, in May, from the two remaining sheds with an active

allocation, Salisbury (70E) and Bournemouth (70F). She remained in store at Nine Elms. The withdrawn engines were taken to Eastleigh to await disposal. Sale having been negotiated, these engines made their last journey, hauled to Briton Ferry in September 1964. They were taken as part of the 03.20 Brighton to Salisbury freight train – in the middle of the night, the better that those of us who loved them, should not see. On 2 September 30107 went; on the 3rd, 30480; on the 9th, 30029; the next night it was the turn of 30057. On 11 September, 30108 made the melancholy journey; finally, on the 15th, went 30667.

I shall not forget my last photograph of an 'M7'. It was 30111. Dumped, and left to rot, outside Nine Elms shed, she was rusting fast when I photographed her on 7 July 1964.

Bad year, 1964.

PLATE 31. Whilst Gresley's restored 'A3' Pacific LNER No. 4472 *Flying Scotsman* preens herself on Eastleigh shed, a much older locomotive stands quietly in the background. Indeed, 4472, built by Gresley in February 1923, was rebuilt to Class 'A3' in 1947, yet was already referred to, at the date of this photograph, 18 May 1963, as a 'veteran'; whilst 'M7' 0–4–4T No. 30251, behind, is more than a quarter of a century older, having entered service on the LSWR in June 1897. No. 30251 was still in BR revenue-earning service when I took this photograph, albeit a mere two months before withdrawal. On the extreme right is Unrebuilt Bulleid 'West Country' Pacific No. 34102 *Lapford*, visiting Eastleigh from Bournemouth. (*previous pages*)

7 North-West Frontier

Notwithstanding my photographs of steam in China, this chapter remains firmly rooted in Britain. Contrary to popular myth, the North-West often sees the sun: that certainly was my experience. The geographic limits of 'North West' for the purpose of this chapter, therefore, encompass an area roughly bounded by Wrexham, Wirral, Merseyside, Preston, Manchester and Warrington: a sausage-shaped swathe of territory once the preserve of GWR, LNWR and L & Y, eventually swallowed up within British Rail's London Midland Region.

Self-discipline dictates that no attempt be made here to write a definitive history of my chosen chapter title. By the time that my response to the call of steam caused me first to enter the North-West Frontier, almost all trace of active GWR steam had been eliminated. Chester and Birkenhead had fallen to the old enemy. Furthermore, the shots I took at Croes Newydd in its death-throes did not reach the final short-list for inclusion in this chapter. In fact, that final choice was made by Obersturmbahnführer Jane Adley, whose vigorous elimination has left eight photographs which truthfully represent the major role left for the steam-engine by the end of 1964; in a word – freight. Of the eight, two were taken at Patricroft, four at Birkenhead and two at Newton Heath. Although each photograph is captioned, collectively they show a range of varied motive-power: worth tabulating out of interest:

Subject	Location	Date
Crab	Newton Heath	3 December 1964
4F + 9F + Black 5 + Ivatt 2MT	Newton Heath	3 December 1964
8F	Patricroft	5 March 1965
BR/STD Class 5 (Caprotti)	Patricroft	5 March 1965
9F	Birkenhead	4 July 1965

Jinties	Birkenhead	4 July 1965
Shed-Scene	Birkenhead	11 July 1965
9F	Birkenhead	9 January 1966

PLATE 32. Ex-Crosti '9F' 2–10–0 No. 92024, seen here taking water on Birkenhead shed on 4 July 1965 reminds me of many happy hours spent at this place. Other motive power on view includes 'Black 5', '8F', 'Crab' and '9F' without Crosti front-end. (*above*)

PLATE 33. The LMS '3F' 0–6–0T commonly known as Jinty was a common sight throughout the north-west from the mid-twenties to the mid-sixties. They personified the LMS. Here, six members of the class enjoy a quiet weekend at Birkenhead shed: Numbers 47272; 47659; 47627 are to the fore. (*top right*)

Whilst Newton Heath was the principal motive-power depot of the Lancashire & Yorkshire Railway, with 170 locomotives allocated in 1950, both Patricroft and Birkenhead were London & North Western territory, albeit the latter owned jointly by LNWR and GWR. How splendid that Jane's selected pictures so well illustrate the traditions of the three sheds.

Newton Heath, in north-east Manchester was host to a very full range of motive power, to cover the numerous and varied duties. By December 1964 the vintage small engines once a familiar sight, such as the L & Y 'F16' Saddle-tanks, had of course long since gone. Local shunting duties were mainly performed by 'Jinties'. How I wish I had been there ten years earlier, when Newton Heath had ten 'Jubilee's operating the shed's top passenger link northwards from Manchester. At that date one would have seen big passenger engines, like the rebuilt 'Royal Scots', which were regular visitors. One might have seen a 'Clan' which would have arrived on a Glasgow to Manchester express. Ah well; even December 1964 provided more varied motive

PLATE 34. There is no mistaking the lines of a BR/Standard '9F' 2–10–0. Whilst a number of the class were built with double blastpipes and chimney, only four were built with single and altered to double later: one of these was No. 92079, seen here climbing cautiously out of her home depot, Birkenhead, on greasy rails on 9 January 1966. (*bottom right*)

PLATE 35. By 3 December 1964, the roof of Newton Heath Shed looked as though it had been attacked by corrugated-iron thieves. Visible, left to right, are LMS '4F' –0–6–0 No. 44247; BR/Std '9F' 2–10–0 No. 92159; 'Black 5' 4–6–0 No. 44818; and Ivatt '2MT' 2–6–0 No. 46418. Note here the splendid water-columns: have any been preserved? (*following pages*)

power than was visible at most other sheds.

Patricroft was unusual; indeed in my experience it was unique through its L shape. Standing in a triangle of lines to the west of the city, the shed's work was linked to the adjacent goods yards (see Chapter 2 *In Search of Steam*). The strange shape came about when the original building was extended in 1904–5, to fit within the triangular piece of land on which it was sited. At the 1923 Grouping Patricroft had an allocation of 120 locomotives; there were about seventy-five on the books in the last few years, mainly covering mixed traffic and freight duties. Patricroft supplied the Miles Platting Bankers, engines I studied closely on my visits to Manchester Victoria.

The four photographs listed above include two significant features of Patricroft's declining years in the 1960s. By this time the shed had become home for many of the Std 'Class 5' 4–6–0s fitted with Caprotti valve-gear. This apparatus was rarely ignored, being either loved or hated by the crews who had to work with it. On the whole, from my conversations, more were 'for' than were 'agin' it at Patricroft. The second feature of the motive-power scene at Patricroft was its role as host to 'Jubilee's and 'Britannia's working into Manchester on trains from North Wales, again illustrated in Plates 37, 38. Patricroft was amongst

PLATE 36. With Manchester again supplying sunshine, my pleasure was completed by the sight of one of my favourite class of locomotive: the 'Crab'. Here, on shed at Newton Heath on 3 December 1964, Hughes-Fowler 2–6–0 No. 42787, a Gorton (9G) engine, has steam to spare as she blows off at 180 lbs per square inch pressure in the boiler. This locomotive was withdrawn in April 1965. (*above*)

PLATE 37. 5 March 1965: one of Patricroft's stud of Caprottis – BR/Standard 'Class 5' 4–6–0 No. 73139, restarts a freight from a signal check, heading north-west past Patricroft MPD. (*right*)

PLATE 38. Hot, still July afternoon in the North West: Birkenhead MPD on 11 July 1965. (*following pages*)

the handful of sheds to survive with steam into high summer 1968.

Birkenhead will always remain a spiritual home for me. As Prospective Conservative Parliamentary Candidate between May 1965 and March 1966 I was very lucky: to learn much, to make friends, and to be able to spend hours and hours at the shed, which I came to know intimately. Perhaps in my next book I can delve more fully into the history of individual sheds. Suffice to say that, with the closure of the ex-LNER depot at nearby Bidston in February 1963, Birkenhead MPD assumed responsibility for the John Summers iron ore trains. By 1966 there were more than fifty '9F' 2–10–0s allocated, along with '8F's, 'Black 5's and a dwindling band of 'Crab's and 'Jinties'.

I hope to have justified this chapter; if you feel I have not done so, see *In Search of Steam*, Chapters 2, 5, 8 and 13. Birkenhead, Newton Heath, Patricroft; and Lostock Hall, Rose Grove, Carnforth; Agecroft, Heaton Mersey, Trafford Park; Longsight and Bank Hall, Dallam and Edge Hill, Chester, Croes Newydd: the last bastions of steam against the infidel invading diesel. North-West Frontier.

PLATE 39. Synonymous with the area was the reliability, imperturbability and strength of the Stanier '8F' 2–8–0, mainstay of LMS and BR freight motive power throughout the region. Visiting Patricroft on 5 March 1965, from neighbouring Heaton Mersey MPD (9F) was '8F' No. 48613. 852 of the class were built between 1935 and 1944, this one being from a batch turned out of Brighton Works in 1943, when a number of non-LMS Works were building standardised locomotives for the national war effort.

8 Midlands

Pusillanimous at best is the choice of title for this chapter. I have had carefully and simultaneously to scrutinise my photographs, my conscience and my old diaries. During my six years – or nearly six years – search for steam to record, my camera was forever by my side. My chosen locations for photography however, were dictated, of necessity, for their proximity to my occupational location. What I am saying, in a rather long-winded way, is that I could only take photographs near where I happened to be, and 'where I happened to be' was determined by my business and social life, neither of which enabled me to make extensive 'photo-vacations' for the sole purpose of railway photography.

Perhaps the largest gap in my arena between 1962 and 1968 was the area covered by this chapter-title. It would be pleasant but fraudulent to write a chapter, without illustration, featuring many of the places I never visited. If only I had been afflicted with the call of steam when living in and travelling extensively from Birmingham in 1953–4. What an opportunity! But I was not: and however distressing are the pangs of unfulfilled ambition, however romantic the conjuring of dreams from words, no literary genius on earth can adequately portray a living picture of an LNWR 'Super D' 0–8–0 at Bescot with a heavy freight, slipping on icy rails early on a freezing January morning, struggling for adhesion whilst hurling towards heaven a cascade of smoke and steam which gushes forth from chimney and blast-pipe, then hangs heavily on contact with the icy air ... ah well.

Where is the Midlands? Which counties does the name encompass? What is a 'county' as opposed to mere con-glomeration? Who shall determine these things? As a Southerner born and bred I must confess a slight disdain for things Midland – not Midland Railway, you understand. Just 'Midland'. The North is strong and witty, the West is best, Scotland and Wales full of character and vitality, the East unknown, flat but fertile:

the Midlands, well – it is just 'between', really. Excuse me – I am not trying to 'do' an A A Milne or Johnny Morris: perhaps the mantle of H V Morton, from whom I plagiarised my title, is slipping over me. I will stop. Where is the Midlands?

The Midlands for purposes of this chapter, takes in the (old) counties of Warwickshire, Worcestershire, Nottinghamshire, Staffordshire, Derbyshire, Leicestershire – AND Rutland. Rutland was and is Rutland. Bryan Matthews at Uppingham would never forgive me if I allowed Rutland to be forgotten, which it will not: or to be conglomerated, which it will not either. My delineation is frankly determined by my very few photographs taken in this area, an area so rich in the history of railways, too.

My initial plans included places as far East as Peterborough and South as Luton: they must find their place elsewhere. It is really the old 'LMS Midlands' that I am able to encompass. Sadly, a depressing visit to Stourbridge when it was in Worcestershire and a 'Hall' on Lickey, are I think the only photography I ever undertook, of GWR engines in my defined area. Discussion of this chapter, and advice sought on the geographical limitations of the Midlands could have included some unlikely places. How often is the proffered answer nothing more than the prejudice of the donor! Thus to someone in rural Wiltshire, Swindon is 'South

PLATE 40. Derby, like Crewe or other railway towns, was likely to offer enthusiasts the sight of engines from widely-scattered locations, visiting for attention at the Works. '9F' 2-10-0 No. 92030, seen here hauling dead '8F' 2-8-0 No. 48270, spent more than eight years based at Annesley, often hauling freights up the Great Central to Woodford Halse. Transferred to Banbury in the twilight of GC operation, she would move again a month after this photograph was taken on 9 September 1966. Her next and final home will be Wakefield (56A) where she survived until withdrawal in February 1967. To the right of London Road Junction Box stand the out-buildings of Derby Works, reached by the long footbridge from which I took this photograph. (Since

Midlands': to the Cornishman, Bristol is Midlands – Swindon is London! To many, Oxford is certainly South Midlands. And what of Bletchley, or Woodford Halse? Perhaps ATV's viewing area is a good guide. Enough: the arbitrary choice is arbitrarily made – delineated by the extent of my meanderings with camera.

Derby, as the home of the Midland Railway, seems the most logical and least controversial place in which to start. For years the Midland Railway pursued a 'small-engine' policy. Justly proud of its reputation for style and standards, successive Chief Mechanical Engineers stuck to a 'home-style' which even its competitors would agree was distinctive. Incorporated in 1844 by the amalgamation of the North Midland, Midland Counties, and the Birmingham and Derby Junction Railway, the continuity of style perhaps flowed from the fact that the MR had but four CMEs throughout its existence, from 1844 to the 1923 grouping. The Midland-style 0–6–0 and 0–6–0T, of '4F' and '3F' respectively, lasted well into the 1960s, a living reminder of a shape and job specification of Midland Railway, and midlands, heritage. At the grouping, following Johnson's standardisation programme, the Midland had only five wheel-arrangements in tender and seven in tank engines. Samuel Waite Johnson indeed, CME from 1873–1903, introduced that magnificent rich distinctive shade of maroon which BR tried to reproduce on the Stanier 'Coronation' Pacifics, some of whose last main-line passenger duties were at Euston's steam swan-song, working expresses to Birmingham and Wolverhampton on the main line of the old Midland's great rival, the London and North Western (LNWR).

On 3 March 1963, the day after my birthday I was at Euston to record, in the late afternoon sun, 'Coronation' Pacific No. 46251 *City of Nottingham* depart with the 16.15 to Manchester Piccadilly: No. 46254 *City of Stoke-on-Trent* with the 16.30 for Wolverhampton: and No. 46248 *City of Leeds* on the Fridays-only 16.45 Euston to Liverpool Lime Street. The sight and sound and feel of these departures remain forever in my memory, aided by photographic evidence of a world long gone.

Whilst dwelling on memories of things midland and Midland, and apologising for the LNWR digression at Euston (this chapter is Midlands, not Midland!) let me take you back to Mr Johnson's 0–6–0s, and 1963. The month following my reverie at Euston, I found myself at Bedford, in that ugliest of engine sheds that is still there. How typical that so much splendid railway architecture should be gone to dust, but this particular piece of brick-boredom should survive. However dull the shed's exterior, the contents were, in the modern idiom, 'something else' (How grim is this all-purpose use of language – just like a Type '4' diesel).

Right at the back of the shed, hiding from the light the emergence into which would inevitably mean the last journey, to the breaker's yard, was a veteran indeed: a Johnson Midland 0–6–0 locomotive from a class introduced in 1885. She was No. 43453.

It was a quiet Saturday afternoon. Having ascertained that the duty foreman was friendly, I tried my luck. 'Didn't expect still to see an old lady like that' I said 'Maybe ancient, but they've got some life left' he replied. 'In fact, in the recent freeze-up, we've been using a couple of them for the freight workings on the Hitchin branch.'

I took the plunge. 'Is there any chance at all of getting her out into the open so that I could photograph her in colour?' 'Hmmm – don't see why not – it's pretty quiet.' Soon the shed came to life. 'Black 5' No. 45416, in steam outside the shed, was mobilised. Backing down slowly on to the left-hand road looking into the four-road shed, she drew up to 43453. With one man in the 'Black 5's cab, another attaching the two locomotives, and a third standing-by, Bedford MPD awoke from its Saturday afternoon slumber. Slowly the dead '3F', protesting somewhat, was eased into the spring sunshine. Recounting this saga nearly 20 years on, I have the photographs to recall that bond of friendship and co-operation between working railwaymen and enthusiasts.

PLATE 41. 'Beneath the wires', north of Stafford on 6 March 1965, a much-travelled 'Black 5' 4–6–0 with steam to spare, plods south with a lengthy rake of empty car-flats. Built for the LMS by Armstrong-Whitworth in 1937, No. 45426 was shedded at Crewe South, Crewe North, Willesden, Northampton, Banbury, Annesley and finally Edge Hill between June '62 and withdrawal in March '68. Photograph taken from an overtaking Manchester–Euston express. Note 'Northampton' – her home shed – painted on buffer-beam.

PLATE 42. Evidence of preparation for electrification is clearly visible at Coventry Station in May 1963. Note the insulated area on the underside of the bridge, just above the dome of BR/Std Class '4' 4–6–0 No. 75052. The engine, based at Nuneaton, bears that shed's 2B shedplate number, changed during 1963 to 5E. From Nuneaton 75052 was transferred away to Holyhead, Machynlleth and finally Stoke, from where she was withdrawn in August 1967.

Leaning his shunter's pole against the end wall of the shed, one of the 'actors' in this minor drama called-on the driver of the 'Black 5' – a grubby member she was, too, with BR Lion rampant on wheel just visible through the grime. But one thing spoils this memory – Gevaert. If only I had been using Kodak film my record today would not be a flat sepia.

I 'shot' the old lady side view, front view, even rear view. The next photographs, a few minutes later, were of LMS '4F' 0–6–0 No. 44540 pulling out of Bedford South Yard, gaining the Midland up slow line, heading south past Bedford (South) Main Box and on over the River Ouse. Even at this date the up slow line by the signal box still sported a splendid relic of Midland Railway signalling. Many of these old signals, and the Ouse Bridge signal boxes, lasted until the closure of the little-used sidings on 17 July 1966.

At the end of LMS days in 1947 Bedford Shed (15D) was, with Leicester and Kettering, a member of the Wellingborough Motive Power area. British Railways in its early years was like China during the cultural revolution: constant change creating great confusion, but of little practical benefit to the general population. Bedford Shed was put under Cricklewood's umbrella. Wellingborough however, 15A and its own master in 1947, was

still thus until September 1963, when it was transferred to the Leicester Division. It remained 15A for a time: then this was altered and it became 15B. One hopes at least that the shed-plate manufacturers benefitted from all this! At Wellingborough in the mid-fifties were located the ten '9F' 2–10–0s fitted with Franco-Crosti boilers, with their ungainly side-chimneys.

By mid 1963 the majority of freight workings on the Midland line south of Wellingborough were diesel-hauled, the passenger services on the main-line having long since succumbed to the oil-enemy. The push-and-pull service between Wellingborough and Northampton was still steam-hauled, by Class '2' 2–6–2T. My camera, sadly Gevaert-filled, recorded Midland '4F' 0–6–0 No. 43995 inside the shed, with her shedplate number (15D) painted on, a phenomenon to which we were soon to become only too accustomed, as thieves got their hands on historic cast-iron before shedmasters became aware of what was happening. 'Jinty' 0–6–0T No. 47273: another MR '4F' 0–6–0, No. 43850 alongside '8F' 2–8–0 No. 48027 with smoke-box door open, inside the roundhouse: and finally, dead but proud, another Johnson Midland '3F' 0–6–0, No. 43342, were recorded for posterity.

Continuing my following of the call of steam around the South Midlands, 'we', as H V Morton might have said 'we come to Northampton.' Here, on 7 July 1963 I managed to obtain a reasonably clear view of a 'Crab' for the first time. These splendid engines, to which I was to become greatly attached by the time they ended their careers in Birkenhead some $3\frac{1}{2}$ years later, were hard to find so far south by this date. Here however was 42723; this time the engine was being manoeuvred around the precincts of the shed by a 'Black 5' in line of duty, not as at Bedford, at my behest. An LNWR shed, Northampton came within the Rugby area, along with Nuneaton and Woodford Halse (see page 110) at the time of my visit. Later that day I reached Peterborough, eastern outpost of the east Midlands but with a different railway heritage which properly precludes its receiving but a mention in this chapter. Mere mention of the place recalls to mind school days at Uppingham, almost equidistant twixt Peterborough and Leicester.

The call of steam 1962–68: Peterborough, Leicester, Uppingham: my days at Uppingham 1948–52 would have been a railway photographer's dream. The branch train to Seaton: Harringworth viaduct: the Tilbury tanks on Uppingham branch trains: and branch trains that did not run. Oh yes! I do recall, one school day at Uppingham, visiting the (out-of-bounds) station and being told 'Seaton doesn't send the train unless one or other of us has a passenger.' Small tank engines and one coach were not intimidated by the steep gradient, 1 in 60 in places. During the

PLATE 43. Late afternoon sun glints on the flank of the boiler of a Midlands-bound express from old Euston. 'Coronation' Pacific No. 46254 *City of Stoke-on-Trent* has the right-away with the 16.30 Birmingham and Wolverhampton express on 3 March 1963. It was the day after my birthday, and the last occasion on which I would photograph a Stanier Pacific at Euston. The last one was condemned in 1964. (*previous pages*)

last year of service, Tilbury tank No. 41975 was a frequent performer on the branch, which lost its passenger service on 13 June 1960, and was closed completely and the track lifted after the withdrawal of freight services and school specials on 1 June 1964.

If pangs of remorse came over me at failing to photograph steam in the rural east Midlands, then my year spent based in Birmingham whilst working for Pearl and Dean in 1954 ranks as my golden era of lost opportunity. The old New Street Station probably deserved Morton's description as a 'grimy conservatory' but that merely makes my loss the greater.

Unless I locate my old diary before I hand over the manuscript for this book to my publisher, the mists of time preclude the functioning of memory to recall the reason for an obviously brief visit to Coventry in May 1963. Jane was with me and we visited the new Cathedral, which left less of an impression on me than the knowledge that steam was fast on the wane. From 24 March the main line between Coventry and Birmingham was closed on Sundays for electrification work. Coventry shed had closed as long ago as 17 November 1958 due to the effect of road haulage on the short-haul freights once the staple traffic of the depot. Although some of the 'Specials' bringing visitors to the Cathedral were steam-hauled – 'V2's from Newcastle, 'B1's from Bishop Auckland – regular local work remaining in the hands of steam was mainly freight, although a 'Black 5' worked the Coventry holiday week 'Holiday Express' to a different resort daily during the week commencing 14 July 1963.

That day in May '63 I photographed BR/Std '4MT' 4–6–0 No. 75052 running Light Engine through the station, the platforms and superstructure of which were already rebuilt for the electric era. In my photograph of 75052 her chimney appears equidistant, as she passes under the overbridge, between the pads which will hold the electric catenaries. The second photograph features Stanier '8F' 2–8–0 No. 48206 entering the station from the Rugby direction, with a ballast train, presumably destined for the electrification work west of Coventry on the Birmingham main line. The junction to Kenilworth is clearly visible: indeed the Perutz film in my camera gave noticeable clarity even on dull days, albeit with a somewhat green tinge.

If Coventry was rarely featured in contemporary railway periodicals such as *Railway Observer*, the excellent and irreplaceable bibliographic source of information for my memory-jogging researches, then Nottingham fared somewhat better. It was on 16 July 1964 that my camera and I first arrived there to photograph steam: and that was both my first and last 'photo-foray'. Nottingham in addition to its justifiable claim to be, with Derby, the hub of the old Midland – the first section of the Midland Counties Railway, the oldest of the three constituent companies of the MR, being opened between Nottingham and Derby in 1839 – was a key location on the Great Central, and an important outpost for the Great Northern too, as that railway probed and established itself westwards from its main line at Grantham. The motive power on Nottingham shed and in the area that day nevertheless reflected the dominance of the Midland/ LMS. If my contemporary ignorance of railway history had not precluded it, a visit to Nottingham should have included a pilgrimage to the Great Central. Only since closure of that fine line, late lamented by its connoisseurs, and superbly recaptured during its swan-song, decline, decay and dereliction by Colin Walker in *Main Line Lament*, have I appreciated what I missed. If you do not possess a copy of *Main Line Lament*, you are poor: for Walker has ensured that whomsoever is not stirred by his tale of the Great Central, is without soul.

Let us get back to Nottingham, 16 July 1964. Oldest locomotive on shed that day was Fowler MR '4F' 0–6–0 No. 43964: at the other end of the time-scale was BR Standard '2MT' 2–6–0 No. 78062, which was turned out of Darlington works in 1956. Also there were two LMS classes, similar in appearance, which rarely attracted attention yet which provided LMS motive power on suburban and intermediate passenger trains throughout that railway's system, namely the Stanier and Fairburn 2–6–4T. The sight of Fairburn tank No. 42221 bringing empty stock into Nottingham Midland Station seemed somehow sad, merely because it was a sight one would not much longer see. Most disturbances to life's pattern bring unwelcome change: some merely unwelcome as a passing inconvenience, just a minor disruption of routine; others presaging such fundamental change that their impending arrival causes deep foreboding, not one whit alleviated when envisaged change occurs. Such was the passing of the steam engine, of which I felt aware at Nottingham.

Where else shall I take you on this Midlands meander? Come with me to the far North of my arbitrarily-delineated area – to Stafford, where, north of the station on a bitingly cold 6 March 1965, I photographed 'Black 5' 4–6–0 No. 45426 hauling empty carflats southbound on the LNWR main line. Snow lay on the ground as I took my shot from an overtaking southbound Manchester–Euston express. No. 45426 although unkempt, had steam to spare, which she blew off defiantly through the overhead electric power supply. Steam clung to her flanks in the cold air as she headed south, perhaps to end up at her home, indicated as 'Northampton' on her buffer-beam. *Railway Observer* for March 1965 notes 45426 as transferred to 1H,

PLATE 44. Rapid dieselisation of suburban and intermediate passenger services rendered obsolete large numbers of pasenger tank locomotives based at Midland sheds. Fairburn 2–6–4T No. 42284, with smoke-box door open, stands forlornly in the near-deserted roundhouse of Nottingham Midland MPD on 16 July 1964.

Northampton, during the four weeks ended 30 January 1965.

Full electric working had been introduced between Rugby and Crewe – including Stafford – on 4 January 1965. Stafford Shed closed on 19 July 1965. There had been an engine shed at Stafford since the 1850s. Indeed, my designation of the place as 'Midlands' rather than 'North' can be justified by the decision of the LNWR in January 1860 to make Stafford 'the limit of both Divisions, *i.e.* Northern and Southern' and 'that an independent Engine shed be erected at Stafford for the Southern Division'. Of the ten locomotives allocated to Stafford shed as at 24 April 1965, just under three months prior to its closure, five were 'Black 5's; there were two '8F's, two 'Jinties' and a Fowler 2–6–4T. Meanwhile electrification work at this date proceeded apace on the line through Stoke-on-Trent. Stations were rebuilt, bridges raised, old signal boxes closed and replaced by new power-boxes: and the steady spread of the steel masts was like the coming of the Triffids.

My photography of steam at Stoke was restricted to three shots in heavy rain on a miserable March day in 1967, from a passing train. None is really worth reproducing: and to a scene at the shed (5D) later that year that looked as though those Triffids had just passed through. Indeed, the notes in my master-catalogue tell their own tale: 'view of just-dead shed': 'dead': 'coal-stage that will deliver no more coal': 'awaiting the final journey'. Stoke shed closed in August, on the 22nd of which month I visited the nearest mechanical equivalent imaginable to an oriental death-house. Engines still at the shed prior to their removal for cutting-up included Stanier 'Black 5' Nos. 44860 and 45050 and '8F's Nos. 48110, 48128/31: Ivatt '4MT' 2–6–0 No. 43115: and BR/STD '4MT' 4–6–0 Nos. 75002/18/71. No. 75071 was of interest as a former resident of Bath (Green Park) MPD.

No. 48128, at the head of a line of forlorn yet recently-active locomotives, was short of smoke-box numberplate, and her smokebox-door was ajar. That apart, she looked, she was, ready and willing to serve for many years. Next, I photographed 75071 inside the roundhouse. A tell-tale oval patch of rust showed whence her 'manufacturer's' plate had been removed. One of the double-chimney members of the class, her smokebox was an extraordinary hue of red rust, so soon after withdrawal. Wandering outside again, I photographed another once-proud member of a famous class: 45050, with connecting-rod removed and, string attached, lying along her running-plate. As the sun emerged, it caught the still-bright red paintwork of the buffer-beam of 75002. By what act of criminal folly did we countenance the wicked waste of millions of useful hours of work remaining in the thousands of steam-engines put to the torch in the sixties?

And so my dismal trek around the shed continued. Even in death these silent friends told of their own existence. No. 75002, still clean in lined-out green, displayed a green disc immediately below her cabside number.

If my memories of the Midlands thus recalled, dwell overmuch on LMS heritage, I am sorry: as mentioned earlier, my only GWR shed photography in the region was at Stourbridge, and the scene awaiting me on 18 July 1966 was little different atmospherically from that recounted at Stoke. Closed to steam just seven days before my visit, the building itself, unlike Stoke, was almost square externally. It was a standard GWR single unit turntable shed, situated half a mile from Stourbridge Junction station. The silent panniers still looked pert. The sun, penetrating through grimy windows, or empty window-frames, silhouetted '57xx's. Intriguing was the style of numerals painted on the cabsides of some of the panniers. No. 9614 still had one of her fire-irons hooked on to her bunker. Indicative of regional change in this part of the Midlands, the silent panniers kept company with an LMS Ivatt 2–6–0 and a Stanier 'Black 5': whilst, in the Repair Shop I photographed BR/STD '9F' 2–10–0 No. 92204 standing forlornly behind the lifting-tackle. Outside the shed, the water-columns stood in voiceless vigil: a bleak LMS trio stood amongst the weeds.

Wandering beyond the confines of this dismal scene of dereliction I headed for the still-proud and still-active GWR lower-quadrant signals, on what was once their sole preserve. The knowledge that GWR steam had been totally eliminated barely reduced my pleasure at the sight and sound that caught my attention. Pulling out of the loop, southwards in the direction of the Junction and Worcester, was a real, live steam engine. Stumbling across the rusty tracks, hurriedly getting my faithful Voigtlander 'at the ready', I captured an unidentified '8F' gaining the main line, as a Brush Type '4' diesel (I think they are called: I do not really care: my only concern was to prevent that featureless box on wheels coming twixt my lens and the 8F) crawled towards adverse signals on the northbound line. Was this the last colour photograph of living steam at Stourbridge?

The closure of Stourbridge shed was not quite the end of the 'Stourbridge Pannier', the long-lived push-and-pull which ran between Junction and Town Stations. A pannier from Tyseley shed provided the motive power, but not for long. Steam was replaced by a single diesel car. From 24 July 1967 Stourbridge Town station was unstaffed for much of the day, tickets being issued by the guard on the diesel car. However, the service between Town and Junction survives, albeit Second Class only and no Sunday service. Unusually, the branch, although double-

track, was in steam days worked as two single lines, one for passenger trains and one for goods. The 14-acre goods-station site a short distance beyond the Town Station had closed the previous July.

GWR panniers, a handful of which staggered into 1966 under Midland Region operation, were the last of the standard-gauge GWR locomotives to remain in service: the withdrawal of '57xx' panniers 4646, 4696 and 9774 from Tyseley during the four weeks ending 3 December 1966 was indeed the end of an era, and not just in the West Midlands.

We have travelled far in this chapter, and seen the decline and fall of steam. I said on page 91 that we would start our meander round the Midlands in Derby, home of the old Midland Railway. We shall end there, too: on 9 September 1966. That day I also visited Burton-on-Trent, photographing steam there for the first and last time, the day after the closure of Burton shed to steam power. One solitary '8F', No. 48367, stood guard inside the roundhouse, as representative an engine as could be imagined. Sturdy, reliable – fine engines, doomed to an early death years before normal life expiry. Nobody would accuse the men of steam of indulging in built-in obsolescence.

Notwithstanding the closure of Burton shed, steam was still in

PLATE 45. 'Black 5' 4–6–0 No. 44841 from Saltley prepares to attack the Lickey Incline with a fitted freight, on a dismal wet 'Summer' day, 6 June 1964. Twenty years on from D-Day, the drama of steam's assault on Lickey, with bankers, much whistling, and crescendos of sound, would soon be but a memory, like the gantry in the picture. Sister engine No. 45310, a pre-war Armstrong, Whitworth-built engine, waits for the road in the loop.

PLATE 46. One week after closure of Stourbridge MPD the Pannier Tanks still in the shed on 18 July 1966 seemed embalmed in time. Soon, they would be gone. Though dead, they were not yet in decay, yet they appeared like unwilling inmates of some oriental death-house. Two members of the once numerous 57xx class, Nos. 9608 and 9614 keep company; a chilling harbinger of the final end of GWR steam.

evidence in the area. Indeed, *Modern Railways* November 1966 noted 'By contrast with other parts of BR, steam workings seem to have increased in the Derby area, particularly on the line from Burton. About 30 per cent, of freights on the Derby-Burton line were noted with steam haulage at the end of September. Trips by NER-based 'B1' 4–6–0s or 'K1' 2–6–0s to the Derby area now appear to be daily turns; they work in with an afternoon freight and the locomotive stables at Derby overnight before returning north early the following day.' Their words are confirmed by my own notes following my visit to the former Midland Railway HQ on 9 September 1966. Of the twelve photographs taken that day, comprising four different classes, only one was an LMS type; the Stanier '8F'. The other types represented were WD 'Austerity' 2–8–0; BR/Standard '9F' 2–10–0; and a 'B1' 4–6–0, No. 61237 *Geoffrey H. Kitson*. Its arrival was doubtless within the framework of traffic movements mentioned above, being allocated to Wakefield MPD at this date. (See page 139.)

No. 61237 incidentally, was one of the eighteen 'B1's named after LNER directors. Forty were named after animals in the antelope family. One only was named following nationalisation in 1948; 61379 was christened *Mayflower* on 13 July 1951 at the request of a society interested in promoting British-American friendship (see page 140, Chapter 12, Kitson Ree & Milne).

Visiting Derby was a special occasion for any railway enthusiast. Historically of outstanding importance, a visit always provided the possibility of seeing rare, unusual or unfamiliar engines. By this date a named 'B1' qualified for special interest and attention, and I knew in my bones that this would be my last visit to a Steam Derby. So it indeed proved to be. No. 61237 became the last LNER engine in steam and in BR service, that I photographed: 90617 similarly the last 'Austerity'. Referring to the Railway Correspondence and Travel Society visit to Derby on 12 March 1967, *Railway Observer* notes 'For the first time no steam locomotives were present and it is understood they are now banned from the Division.'

Wending my weary way home that September day I stopped off at Banbury for another 'final visit'. The shed there was within a month of closure. As the early autumn light faded, the sight of three 'Black 5's simmering on shed epitomised an era ending. They looked as though they knew ... The driver of '8F' No. 48669 inspected his steed by the shed's turntable. Someone, despairingly, defiantly had spruced up the cabside number plate of 'Black 5' No. 45132. Ivatt '2MT' 2–6–0 No. 46522 was standing, dead, outside the shed. Finally, perhaps a portent of the preservation age to come, perhaps as a reminder that LNER as well as LMS and GWR, not to mention their forebears, were involved in the Midlands, there rested in the lifting-shop 'B1' No. 61306. I saw this engine nearly two years later, on my last visit to Carnforth BR shed on 25 June 1968. Now she is restored and running on the latter-day Great Central Railway, Loughborough.

The steam railway was totally identified with the Midlands. In truth no preserved railway scene can ever recapture the spirit of steam. Indeed with steam's decline and disappearance, the Midlands are diminished: but where is not ...

9 The Train Not Standing On Platform 2

Of course we miss the steam-engine. But we have lost much more beside, these last twenty years. As discussion still rages about what should, or should not be done to, with or for the remaining engines at Woodhams, Barry (see Chapter 15), and the viability of current or projected preservation projects is discussed, my mind dwells not just on the locomotives we have lost, but on the stations, indeed one might say on the railways themselves.

Inevitably the conflict between 'Railway Mania' construction in the era of the horse, and railway rationalisation in the era of the motor-car, would result in closures of lines that to many people were their only rail-link. Indeed the demise of the Great Central Railway meant more than the severance of communications: for a place like Woodford Halse it was akin to the death of a community. Whilst the competition engendered by the era of 'Railway Mania', was usually to the benefit of the travelling public, it cannot be said that all rationalisation has resulted in equivalent benefits to all travellers. Shrewsbury citizens may well have preferred seven through services daily to Paddington, than three to Euston.

Some of the stations that have disappeared from the railway map must once have seemed permanent, timeless and indestructible. Whilst Morton Pinkney may be remembered by few and mourned by less, that cannot be said, surely, of Glasgow St Enoch or Buchanan Street; Birmingham Snow Hill, Birkenhead Woodside, or Manchester Central, to name but five. With the closure of termini and whole railway systems, as well as the elimination of innumerable steam motive power depots, we have lost an important part of Britain's architectural heritage. My only minor consolation is that some of my colour photographs have become historic records as a result of this pruning. If only I had had the wit to pay as much attention to the buildings as I did to the engines – who knows: I might have managed a literary effort devoted exclusively to railway architecture! As it is, this chapter

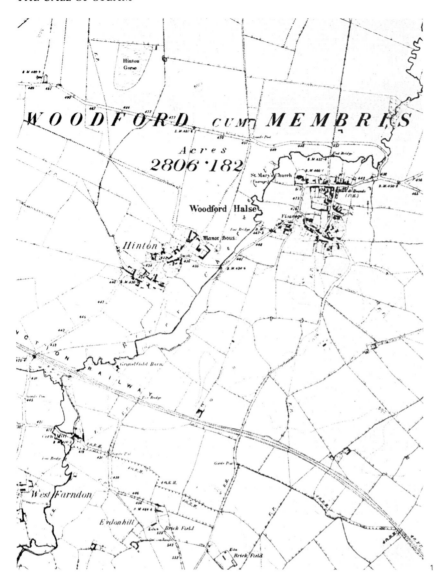

Fig. 12 (page 106) Fig. 13 (page 107) Fig. 14 Fig. 15 (page 108)

Woodford. Four maps that tell an astonishing tale, detailed in words in the accompanying chapter. On the first Ordnance Survey map dated 1882, the village of Woodford Halse has no railway, but is close to the East and West Junction Railway, seen passing to the south of Hinton. On map no. 2, dated 1899, the Great Central Railway has well and truly arrived, with its double junction on a triangle of land with the East and West Junction; by this date the Stratford-on-Avon and Midland Junction Railway (SMJ). By 1955, the date of map no. 3, Woodford's major railway significance is clear. By 1980, all that remains is white space, superimposed on which is the tell-tale phrase 'Dismantled Railway'.

must suffice, with its incidental illustrations of buildings long since either flattened or at best derelict. Please excuse the fact that even the photographs selected to accompany this chapter, are really pictures of locomotives to which the attendant buildings – at the time and in the intention of the photographer – were merely background. That realisation only adds to the bittersweet nostalgia, the feeling of regret and despair that accompanies any realisation of lost opportunities which life can never again offer.

Hopefully the captions to the photographs, and the accompanying maps and diagrams, may help to rekindle memories. Of all the locations at which I photographed steam's decline, none now seems more mournful than Woodford Halse. The birth of the

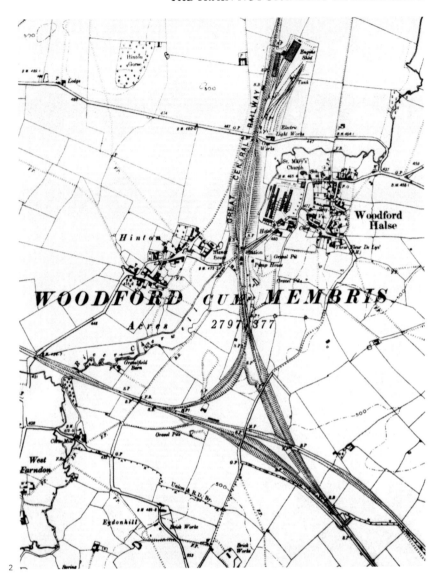

Great Central has been well enough recorded and documented. For the parish of Woodford-cum-Membris however, the railway was more than the creation of a transport link, it was the birth of a new and unknown era. Where rural stability had reigned, in this quiet quarter of Northamptonshire, all was transformed. At the 1851 census, the parish population was shewn as 455. By 1891 it had risen merely to 527. Forty years would have wrought little scenic change. Yet in the census of 1901 – just over a year following the opening of the Great Central – Woodford-cum-Membris parish population showed an increase of 230 per cent on the figure ten years earlier. Now, 1220 souls inhabited this thriving railway outpost. The Great Central built rows of terraced houses. Ten years later, another 300 was added to the population

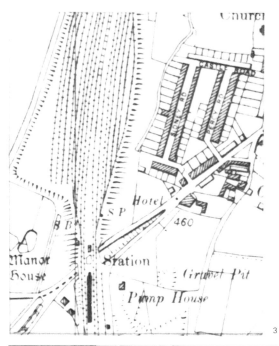

3

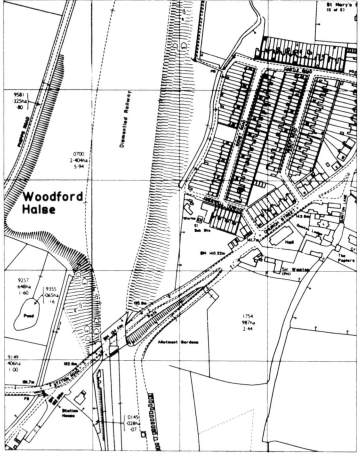

4

MICROGRAPH IV. When
reading my eulogy of
Woodford Halse, Derek Cross
was blunt: 'I like the
nostalgia of this – especially
as I have not a clue where
Woodford Halse is (or was) or
indeed why it or the G.C.'s
London Extension was ever
built. (Apart from the bloody
mindedness of Watkin).'
Once again, Bill Tasker
solved my problem, by
producing from his archives
the perfect map – entitled
AREA MAP OF
BIRMINGHAM DISTRICT
OUTDOOR MACHINERY
ENGINEER. From this map I
have extracted an area
centred on Woodford – just
for the benefit of Derek
Cross. That is the least I can
do for a chum who reads a
manuscript and tells you
what he really thinks, rather
than what he thinks you
really want to hear.
(opposite)

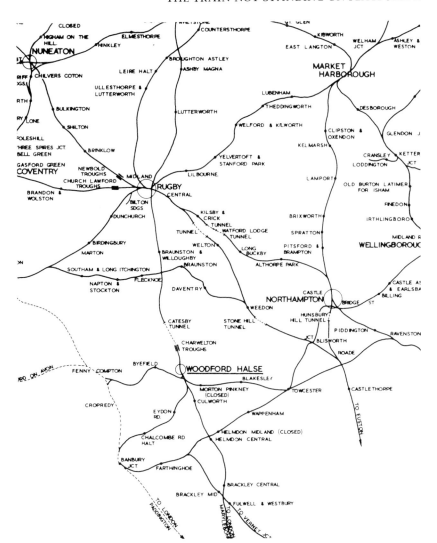

MICROGRAPH V. (Page 112)
My only regret is the absence
from this chapter of a
photograph I took of a 'B1'
4–6–0 at Manchester Central
with the 23.05 to Marylebone
one night in March 1963.
Manchester Central Station
opened, after a lengthy and
stormy birth, on 1 July 1880,
and closed on 5 May 1969.

The city was perhaps the
first major urban growth
attributable to the Industrial
Revolution, and
consequently was an object
of study and interest as a
phenomenon, well beyond its
boundaries. Thus the city has
a legacy of excellent maps
and plans of the large estates
that were such a determining
feature of its railway growth.

Plans of the great termini
yield a wealth of detail: my
eye is attracted not only by
the subject of this drawing –
elevation of screen and facia
boarding – but also by the
beautiful script at the top.
CLC both dates and defines
Manchester Central's
heritage . . .

at the taking of the census: due entirely to the Railway.
Thereafter, growth into the twenties and thirties was steady. Yet
Woodford remained a village: a strange, isolated community,
whose existence was inextricably linked to the railway.

Perhaps, in years to come, when Ordnance Survey terminology
changes, terms like 'Railway Settlement Site' will denote places
like Woodford Halse. Notwithstanding its modernity in terms of
main line construction, the Great Central as a trunk route led a
precarious existence. Following nationalisation, transfer from
Eastern to London Midland regional control in 1958 broke the
link from Great Central to LNER to Eastern Region continuity.
Woodford remained a point of regional interchange, particularly
via Banbury and the Western Region. Yet as elsewhere on BR,
change of regional control often brought lines under the
jurisdiction of erstwhile competitors. In retrospect, the very

success of the Annesley to Woodford freights between these two important marshalling-yards, represented the Great Central's last gasp of main-line existence. The summary termination of the 'windcutters' or 'runners' as they became known, in June 1965, after the passenger service had already been reduced to a mere insult, drained away the life-blood from the line.

My only visit to Woodford Halse was on a truly filthy day, 6 June 1964. It rained continuously, the light was dismal for colour photography, and the meteorological mood was matched by the aura of dank depression on the Great Central. It was a year before complete closure of Woodford yards and shed, yet the writing was on the wall: I can still remember even at that date, the high proportion of 'For sale' notices on the houses in this strange place, that by now had an air of foreboding about it. My companion that day was Ed Chilton, at that time a director of the Rank Organisation. I have not seen Ed, or spoken to him for a very long time, and wonder if his memories remain as strong as do mine.

The act of writing this chapter has not merely brought back memories, it has stirred me to catalogue, and to transfer from negative to positive film, the few colour photographs I took on Kodacolour. The act of scrummaging and scavenging around for all those scruffy pieces of paper on which I noted my

PLATE 47. Clearly the dilapidated state of Woodford Halse's shed buildings indicate their early demise. 6 June 1964 was an utterly dismal day. Whilst colour photography in these conditions, even with the fastest film then available, was not conducive to an attractive end-product. I do not regret my determination to record the dying days of a once-proud railway centre. Fairburn 2–6–4T No. 42251 presides over the dereliction. (above)

PLATE 48. Not just the engine: the platform: the wall: the station canopy – everything here is but a memory. Fairburn 2–6–4T No. 42247 is about to depart from Birkenhead Woodside with the 2.35 train to Paddington, on a Friday afternoon in June 1965. (right)

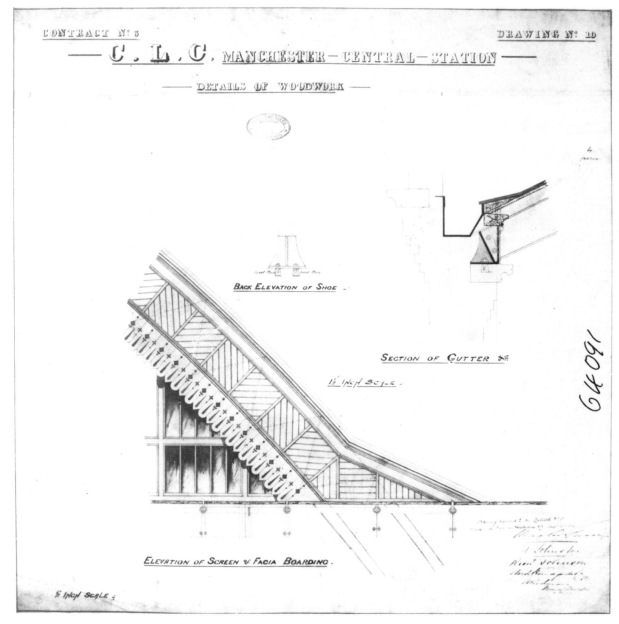

CAPTION: See page 109

photographs, is marvellous! It took me two weeks to find the negatives. That wet June day in 1964 we also visited Bromsgrove and the Lickey Incline, and Honeybourne, another erstwhile railway junction and place of activity, which name features no more in BR timetables. Let me not start to ramble on about Honeybourne, or else this chapter will never end. I return instead to Woodford, nudged into so doing by the writing of the word 'timetable'.

Fortunately I have kept my old timetables from the end of the steam era. One look at the passenger service on the Great Central

PLATE 49. The artistry of the cartographer is superbly illustrated by this Ordnance Survey hand-tinted map of Manchester, showing the area around Central Station. The map is dated 1894. (*right*)

from London out to and through Woodford, and on to Rugby Central, Leicester Central and Nottingham Victoria, tells as good a tale as any as to why trains no longer stand at their platforms or indeed why there are no platforms there. Midland Region did their best to ensure their ability to justify closure, by providing a passenger service timed to be convenient to few. From Marylebone in the timetable dated 9 September 1963 to 14 June 1964 the 4.38 pm to Brackley, Woodford and stations to Nottingham (those that were left) was just early enough to be uncatchable by any potential commuters. The next train from Marylebone was the 9.55 pm, due Woodford at 11.46 pm! Page 516 of that timetable tells its own story of the Great Central under the tender care of BR Midland Region.

In the timetable dated 14 June 1965 to 17 April 1966 the station closures above were no longer mentioned. The Great Central was on its knees. The last passenger train ran on Saturday 3 September 1966. Twenty-seven years to the day from the outbreak of World War II, Beeching succeeded where Hitler had failed. Woodford, which as a thriving railway centre had seemed an indelible part of the landscape, expired. If the Great Central line had survived, Woodford Halse might have usurped the role allocated to Milton Keynes.

PLATE 51. A scene of utter dereliction is all that remains today at Highbridge S & D Station. Not only the engine, signals, platform and track have gone – the Somerset & Dorset Joint Railway has been obliterated – in all but memory, which will never fade. Still sporting an LMS face, Ivatt 2–6–2T No. 41214 pulls away from Highbridge on 20 February 1965, with the 14.20 train to Templecombe. (*above*)

PLATE 50. A symbol of a great railway: the GWR's St Philips Marsh roundhouse, Bristol. Inside, proud and erect, on 26 January 1963, stand No. 4955 *Plaspower Hall* and No. 7815 *Fritwell Manor*, visitors from Taunton and Carmarthen respectively. There was an ethereal calm about the big shed. (*opposite*)

THE CALL OF STEAM

Ilmer Halt Haddenham (Bucks)	Stations are closed; the locality is served by buses of the City of Oxford Motor Services.
Quainton Road Calvert	Stations are closed; the locality is served by buses of the City of Oxford Motor Services and Red Rover Bus Co.
Finmere	Station is closed; the locality is served by buses of the City of Oxford Motor Services and United Counties Omnibus Co.
Helmdon Whetstone	Stations are closed; the locality is served by buses of the Birmingham and Midland Motor Omnibus Co.
Charwelton	Station is closed; the locality is served by buses of the Birmingham and Midland Motor Omnibus Co., and K. W. Coaches Ltd.
Belgrave & Birstall Rothley Quorn & Woodhouse	Stations are closed; the locality is served by buses of the Birmingham and Midland Motor Omnibus Co., and Trent Motor Traction Co. Ltd.
Rushcliffe	Halt is closed; the locality is served by buses of the South Notts. Bus Co. Ltd.
Ruddington	Station is closed; the locality is served by buses of the Trent Motor Traction Co. Ltd., and Barton Transport Co. Ltd.
Arkwright Street	Station is closed; the locality is served by buses of the City of Nottingham Transport Department and West Bridgford Urban District Council Transport Department.
Bulwell Common	Station is closed; the locality is served by buses of the City of Nottingham Transport Department and Trent Motor Traction Co. Ltd.
Hucknall Central	Station is closed; the locality is served by buses of the Trent Motor Traction Co. Ltd., East Midland Motor Services Ltd., and Midland General Omnibus Co. Ltd.
Kirkby Bentinck	Station is closed; the locality is served by buses of the Midland General Omnibus Co. Ltd., and Trent Motor Traction Co. Ltd.
Tibshelf Town	Station is closed; the locality is served by buses of the Midland General Omnibus Co. Ltd.

In those timetables from which I have quoted, Birkenhead Woodside still survived with through trains to Paddington. Paddington! you ask, in the London Midland timetable? Precisely so: and it was not long before my photographs of this old station were to become merely of historic interest. So much has gone, I am just being sentimental. I remember the glory of St Philips Marsh roundhouse in Bristol – on the site of which now is an utterly featureless warehouse or something equally nasty. Even the language has changed, the appreciation of landscape that went with, indeed vitally affected, the steam railway. In the era of HSTs and motorways, who talks of the Northampton Uplands? It was an era, the days of steam, where men had to know the countryside through which the railway passed. Not any more. The train is not standing on Platform 2 at Woodford . . .

Page 519 of the 'Passenger Services Timetable' London Euston St. Pancras Marylebone Broad Street, 9 September 1963 to 14 June 1964.

10 Arnold Walter Hiscock

'Most of them don't know how to handle the "Nelson"'s. Preservation people like to hear the bark of the chimney, and see lots of smoke. I don't agree with that – not at all. A locomotive should be treated like a sewing-machine.' Thus spoke the Eastleigh man whose regular engine as a top-link fireman, prior to promotion to driver, was Eastleigh-based SR 4–6–0 No. 30850 *Lord Nelson*. He was commenting on reports emanating from Carnforth where, at Steamtown, No. 850 has been fully restored and certificated to run again on BR metals.

Born in Eastleigh on 21 August 1920, Arnold Hiscock has steam in his veins. His late son-in-law was also an Eastleigh driver, and his grandfather was employed in the works there. Joining the Southern Railway on leaving school at 17 years of age on 13 March 1938 he climbed the ladder of promotion from cleaner, passed fireman, fireman and was finally promoted to the full rank of engine driver 'about 1950'.

We were having breakfast at Brockenhurst, where he had just brought in the 07.31 from Lymington Pier, on Friday September 25, 1981. In between this and his next duty, the 08.41 from Brockenhurst back to Lymington, he allowed me to 'interview' him in the buffet/refreshment room. It was neither a difficult nor onerous task, although his natural reserve and modesty led him initially to doubt that he could tell me 'anything interesting'.

In the relationship between the engineman and his locomotive: and between engineman and railway company prior to nationalisation – and indeed since – lies one of the seeds of the growth of the very special atmosphere generated by 'the Railway'. Innumerable attempts have been made to define this relationship over the last 150 years: yet none has succeeded in explaining what makes a railway enthusiast. We are born, not made. There must be something in the genes to encourage the generation of immediate rapport between untold combinations of individuals whose normal lives and occupations, outside the

railway interest, would make it unlikely that they met, or communicated, or struck up instant yet lasting friendship.

Life is nothing without personal relationships generated along its path. Most railwaymen that I know and have known, are full human beings. Arnold Hiscock is no exception. His knowledge of gardening: interest in the countryside: pleasure in walking: activity in such subjects as first-aid – the list is endless. An active member of BREL Society (British Rail Engineering Ltd) he leads a full and active life both within and outside his continuing railway employment. Yet, truth to tell, his life has been diminished by the demise of steam. He willingly admits the truth of his wife's remark in 1967, when steam was eliminated on the Southern Region – 'they've taken half your life away from you.' Adding wryly that his wife did not miss the dirty overalls only emphasises that cleanliness can mean sterility of mind as well as body, for the dedicated man of steam.

Eastleigh steam shed at that time, like innumerable others from Thurso to Long Rock, was a veritable nest of active humanity. Full of rich characters, the place was simultaneously workshop, club, society: a nest of men with a strong sense of history, with so many shared interests. Modelling, gardening – 'other drivers

PLATE 52. Arnold Walter Hiscock.

118

taught me about budding roses and grafting fruit trees,' in a phrase, the men were 'interested in life'.

A.W.H. knows that he has been diminished by the demise of steam. He describes superbly the translation of an erstwhile steam motive power depot, into today's electric depot. 'It's like a seaside resort that was a family place where you all went to enjoy the natural things, which has become commercialised, and the relationship, especially between management and man, has gone likewise.'

Our conversation had begun on an operational, not philosophical note. His catalogue of locomotives he had fired and driven, spanned the years, from Victorian engines, to the ultimate manifestation of Southern steam, the Bulleid Pacifics, and finally to the BR 'Standard' classes. He knew his mind; and had his individual likes and dislikes, too. He ran through his memories: 'B4's to 'MN's. I scribbled as he recollected.

'"02": "M7" – that was a good little engine: the old "700"s: then there were the "A12"s and the "Jubilees". We used to run down the Fawley road with them, then back tender first. They had an open tender, and that was pretty draughty sometimes, I can tell you.' He recalled the '0395' class of 0–6–0, and then the 'T9's. Ah, the 'T9's. Clearly he related to Drummond's fine 4–4–0s as one might talk of one's favoured relatives. '117 was the best – the best of them all.' He ran on through the list as each class came to mind, and I scribbled frantically. 'There were the "K10", "L11", "L12", "S15", "N15", "School"s – my favourite engine, the "Schools". No doubt about that. How terrible to paint them black. I had the "Nelson"s of course, and the Bulleid Pacifics – "Merchant Navies" and "West Countries". The rebuilt Bulleids were better engines: you had more control over the valves.'

He then ran through the BR Standard engines he had driven: '76xxx', '75xxx', '73xxx', '82xxx' and 'the "41"s – you know, the little Midland tanks.' Then he mentioned South Eastern and Chatham locos – 'U's, 'N's, 'L1's: the 'Brighton' tanks 'E1', 'E4', 'E5' and 'those Brighton Moguls'. '"K"s I prompted. 'Yes: we used to do the Chichester freight turn with those locos: they were good engines.' He recalled also the LBSC 'C2X' class with their double domes – 'looked a bit like a camel and ran like one, too! Mind you,' he chuckled 'we had some bad engines too. Those "Q"s were never popular. I remember 30532, one of the worst of the lot.' He chuckled again: 'I've got a grim reminder of 30532 – I've made a model and given it that number' he said, revealing yet another hobby needing skill and patience.

'Some of those "Q"s were bad engines. We used to do the Saturday Lymington Branch turn with the through train from Waterloo. The main line loco would come off at Brockenhurst,

and we worked down the branch. If we had set the Forest on fire you can be sure we had a "Q".'

Reminiscence was flowing fast. He was very sorry to see the end of the 'old road' – the original line that went north-westwards from Brockenhurst, across the Forest to Ringwood and down to Poole. This brought him back to the 'M7' tanks – 'good little engines' he repeated. He told me that 127 was his regular engine – or as near as he came to having a regular engine, with the variety of duties and motive power at Eastleigh. He recalled working his 'M7' on the Eastleigh/Portsmouth/Fareham/Romsey lines. 'It was take water here, take water there: run round here, run round there.'

This line of thought about 'M7's brought him on to the subject of fuel conservation. The 'M7' was not so much a thirsty engine, merely one with a limited capacity, built when water in abundance was available at the frequent stops for which the class was originally designed in the 1890s (see Chapter 6). Running out of water was a 'Form One Job' – i.e. the charge sheet. He told me how he nearly 'did it' on an 'M7', when his mate forgot to top up the tanks. Luckily they were in Eastleigh yard at the time. He liked the 'M7' for passenger work, but not on freight duties, tasks for which they were not designed by Drummond, but on which

PLATE 53. His favourite engine and he was not alone in that choice. By the time I started to photograph steam's declining years, Maunsell's 'Schools' Class 4–4–0s had just been withdrawn. No. 30911 *Dover* languished in Hove goods-yard from December 1962 to July 1963, before being scrapped at Eastleigh Works in September. Number plate vandalism was not yet rife by the date of my photograph, 5 May 1963 at Hove. What splendid engines.

PLATE 54. One day he will go to Carnforth to meet again his steed of yesteryear. A coal-eater she may be but Carnforth seems to know how to make her run. Arnold Walter Hiscock's last regular firing was on 'Lord Nelson' 4–6–0 No. 30850 *Lord Nelson.* at Eastleigh. Now returned to main-line condition, No. 850 approaches Appleby with the Cumbrian Mountain Express on 5 August 1981.

they were sometimes used in their latter years. 'Treacherous for brakes' as A.W.H. put it.

Naturally, much top link passenger work came his way. He was fully conversant with the road from Waterloo to Weymouth, but never worked over the Weymouth-Castle Cary line. Inter-regional passenger driving took him over the DNS from Southampton: and he had been far afield on freight work, with 'foreign' motive power. He had driven GWR '28xx' and '38xx' 2–8–0s on the DNS; and to Westbury via Chandlers Ford and Salisbury. 'I've had "Manor"'s, those Collett 0–6–0s, and LMS "8F"'s, on Fawley tanks from Eastleigh. We had a regular turn through to Bletchley with Fawley tanks bound for Northampton: and to Banbury with the sugarbeet trains to Kidderminster.'

But his fondest memories – even above his driving days – were clearly reserved for his firing days on 850 – *Lord Nelson*. She was his regular engine at the end of his time as a fireman. We fell to reminiscing about the old engine now so painstakingly, lovingly, superbly and efficiently restored to main-line working order, and heaving heavy passenger trains, fully laden, not over her familiar terrain of the SW main line but across the steep bleak fells of Cumbria.

850 is *his* engine. He is glad she has been restored, but deep

121

down wonders whether alien drivers and firemen in a northern environment really know how to handle Maunsell's masterpiece. Tales of inexperienced firing, of being thrashed, have clearly reached his ears. One day he will go to Carnforth, to meet again his steed of yesteryear. Meanwhile he frets for her, as though for some long departed soul-mate whose welfare remains a sullen lingering concern.

It is 8.30 am now: time for departure, time to break into our reverie of steam times past. We could have conversed on and on. Arnold Walter Hiscock is a man interested in life, involved in life: a railwayman through and through. There is no higher accolade, for railwaymen are professionals, dedicated to their task, not serving time but fulfilling a calling. A.W.H. has heard and responded to the 'Call of Steam'. . . .

PLATE 55. Entering Eastleigh MPD on 18 May 1963 is Class 'U' No. 31627. A long-time resident of Guildford, and one of the last of the class to remain in service, her routine visit to AWH's home would have attracted little attention.

11 Cross-Country

There was something quite special about our cross-country lines. Indeed, and astonishingly, many rail services still in existence owe their survival more to the history of our railway system, than to the logic of modern travel patterns: only recently did I note the details of the Leeds to Morecambe service, clearly a link straight back to the Midland Railway. The charm of some cross-country routes lay in their independent existence, a few surviving even the 1923 Grouping. Undoubtedly the most celebrated cross-country line was the Somerset and Dorset Joint Railway (SDJR). Quickly, initials flash across one's mind – SMJ: M & GN: DNS: MSWJ: railways born of the determination of individuals, either to put their town on the railway map: or to create a 'missing link' that would open up some hitherto-undreamed-of transport artery: or yet to make a fortune for some opportunist entrepreneur riding on the wave of civic pride so often generated by the early railway schemes.

The cross-country lines, unlike the rail arteries from London and the main provincial cities, were personal and friendly in concept and style: a way of life perhaps, rather than a transport artery. Perhaps it is worth reflecting that, as the motorway network radiates predictably from London and encompasses our major cities, even today many cross-country journeys are made on poor roads. Now sadly, there is no direct rail alternative – from Oxford to Cambridge, from Birkenhead to Bournemouth, from Dumfries to Stranraer.

By the time I responded to the 'Call of Steam', late in 1962, and indeed by the time I educated myself into an awareness of the state of British Rail's steam-hauled services it was almost too late for me to capture any cross-country steam. Family visits to Jane's parents in Burnham-on-Sea gave me access to Highbridge, where branch-line services were still provided to Glastonbury, Evercreech Junction and Wincanton. Ivo Peters' books on the S & D are magnificent historic records: meagre are my efforts to record the last vestiges of life on this incomparable cross-country railway.

By an odd quirk, my first photographs on the S & D at Highbridge included shots of Ivatt 2–6–2T No. 41304: whilst a visit to my parents in Hove provided an opportunity to capture No. 41324 of the same class at Hove on a Brighton to Horsham working. Both these engines were in fact built after nationalisation: 41304 at Crewe and 41324 amongst the final batch, at Derby. By this time these attractive and useful little locomotives had become the basis of the new BR Standard Class '2' 2–6–2T, in the '84xxx' series. The only significant differences between the Ivatt LMS version, some of which were allocated to the Southern Region when new, and the BR machine, were the inclusion of the BR standard fittings such as boiler-feed clack valves in place of LMS-type top-feed, and external regulator rodding. Although ideal for branch and light cross-country services, the spread of the diesel rail-car and the closure of many lines for which they were ideal, overtook the '84xxx' at an early date. Only thirty were built, and the first withdrawal took place in 1963, a mere ten years after introduction.

Thinking about cross-country services one's memory dwells on the engines that handled the light duties. Yet of course many cross-country lines handled long-distance passenger services, and freight, too. By October 1963, the Pines Express, which had been expelled from its traditional S & D route a year previously, was running up the South Western main line, from Bournemouth as far as Basingstoke whence it took the Reading line. This section of its journey was the only stage between Bournemouth and Manchester that was not undertaken on a trunk line. Aware that inter-regional trains used this line, but unaware of precisely what to expect, I kept vigil by the lineside on a moist misty October day in 1963, near Mortimer. As I waited with the patience that was an essential concomitant of steam railway photography in the latter years, my mind drifted idly into imagining the creation of this cross-country link between the GWR at Reading and the LSWR at Basingstoke, opened on 1 November 1848.

Suddenly my dreaming was interrupted by sound: the sound of steam: the noise that was but one factor in the call of steam. Emerging from the mist was an unrebuilt Bulleid Light Pacific, with a substantial train in tow. Poor light and colour film slow by today's standards were constraining factors – to pan or not to pan – split-second decision – click. As she passed I knew that the identity of the train would be known to me long before awareness of the success of the photograph. No. 34041 *Wilton* was in pretty good external condition, and the driver acknowledged my presence with a friendly nod and grin. It was the northbound

PLATE 56. Perhaps the most famous cross-country long-distance train was the Pines Express, for so many years the pride of the S & D. Re-routed away from the ill-fated S & D at the end of the Summer service in 1962, the train ran from Bournemouth via Basingstoke and Reading to Oxford and northwards to Manchester. On 10 October 1963 an unkempt, unrebuilt 'West Country' Pacific, No. 34041 *Wilton* approaches Mortimer with the northbound Pines Express. This was one of the few occasions on which I set out deliberately to photograph a particular train, but the overcast weather did not help me too much.

Pines Express. . . . Mortimer may not be Midsomer Norton but I had captured a piece of railway history. By an odd coincidence *Wilton* was at one time shedded at Bath (Green Park) and was a regular performer on the proper 'Pines Express' via the S & D.

North-South links twixt GWR and LSWR proliferated: in addition to the line through Mortimer, and the S & DJ, there was that strange but delightful line, the Midland and South Western Junction Railway, linking with GWR at Andoversford near Cheltenham, and with LSWR at Andover. Southampton was the target destination for many of these routes – both completed lines and those which reached the stage of Parliamentary approval – or not, as the case may be! How I wish that I had been in the House in the era of the Railway Mania!

My camera never recorded an MSWJ train, but good fortune came my way at Didcot, starting point of yet another splendid dream that, against enormous odds, saw the light of day and survival. Indeed, the Didcot Newbury and Southampton Railway (DNS) epitomised the adventure, the determination, the civic pride, the folly, the inexperience, the malice and the eventfulness that so epitomised the cross-country railway. This is not a history-book, and history may not be your subject, but the story of a railway like the DNS is a microcosm of England's social history.

125

PLATE 57. GWR locomotive, SR coaches, bull-nose track, telegraph-poles and England's green and pleasant land, epitomise the cross-country railway. Steam seemed right and proper in such surroundings, as evidenced by No. 7824 *Iford Manor* threading the Surrey countryside in the Dorking area on a Reading to Redhill working on 20 July 1963. The engine had strayed far from her home, being allocated at this time to Oxley (Wolverhampton) MPD. (*left*)

By 17 July 1965, the DNS was in its death-throes. Great Western engines no longer burst out of the tunnel at Winchester Chesil Station: nor did anything else for that matter. All that remained was the odd stump of track: engineers trains perhaps, to remove whatever was worth collecting. Life was giving way to death: activity to archaeology. In a few years, countryside embankments and perhaps overgrown cuttings will constitute the sole remaining evidence of existence. Anyway I had not come to Didcot to mourn the demise of the DNS, but to ponder the fate of the Great Western shed. I recalled a photograph of Jane in the cab of a '28xx', and the majestic sweep of a 'Castle' round Didcot east curve on a Paddington to Oxford express a couple of years ago. Amazement overcame me at the sight of an engine still 'on shed', if one could use the term to describe what was left of a building. Yet there she was – No. 6928 *Underley Hall*, undoubtedly the last BR-owned engine on shed, and officially withdrawn in June 1965. Naturally I took her photograph, as well as a shot of the shed. As yet, the Great Western Society's plans for Didcot were merely a twinkle in someone's eye. I was only to discover on researching this chapter that that was to be the last GWR tender-engine that I should ever photograph before the Preservation era. (Croes Newydd yielded 0–6–2T and 0–6–0PT the following March, whilst Stourbridge offered dead panniers in July.) Dead of course: steam at Didcot was already but a memory.

Now, few railway photographers can put hand on heart and say 'I never trespassed.' The short-cut to the shed: an illicit line-side photo-call in cutting or by tunnel-mouth: there was rarely the likelihood of apprehension with malice. That was my experience. What one tried to avoid was the blatant crossing of an important and busy main line, in sight of signal-box and station. The need must be paramount: at Didcot that day it certainly was! There was *steam* on the horizon. it was moving. Slowly. Towards me.

I do not know whether Sir Peter Parker will read this book: or, if he does, will issue instructions for the author to be prosecuted for trespassing, but the sight of what transpired to be Stanier '8F' 2–8–0 No. 48662 coming slowly off the DNS towards the GWR main line, was not something I was prepared to observe from afar. I pounded purposefully across the multiple tracks, and just managed to place myself in position to capture the shot in Plate 58.

Use of the phrase 'off the DNS' to describe a photograph taken on 17 July 1965 will raise doubts in the minds of knowledgeable historians, about its authenticity. Although a diverted Pines Express was noted on the line in May 1964 following a derailment at Reading West, the Southern section of the DNS was scheduled to close first; it struggled on for a few more weeks, when the whole through line was closed on 9 August 1964. A GWR Mogul was noted as motive power for the final train on the line, an Eastleigh freight. Transfer trips from Eastleigh to Winchester lingered on until 2 April 1966.

What then was a train doing on the DNS in July 1965? And how on earth did an '8F' get there? Although '9F' 2–10–0s had been seen frequently on the line in the years prior to closure I have never seen another photograph of an '8F': or even heard of the class in use on the line, other than one mention, once. But, 48662 it was – I was there! Detailed, lengthy and diligent scrutiny of the history of this engine has produced only the evidence that it was allocated to Burton (16F) as at 24 April 1965, with no evidence of transfer before 17 July that year.

Time has dimmed neither the memory of the occasion, nor the recognisable features of the photograph. Running, briefly, parallel with the GWR main line through the featureless edge of the town of Didcot, the line swung away sharply southwards. Comparing the Ordnance Survey Seventh Series on which map the DNS line and its stations are very much extant and open, with the current OS map, with its 'Course of old railway' as a dotted line, it is clear that the line itself, and now its course, formed and still form Didcot's eastern boundary. Amongst my many rewards of railway enthusiasm is a letter received from Harold Gasson, former GWR fireman and now author, whose reminiscences of life on the DNS are a joy to read.

Unlike Harold Gasson or indeed the great O S Nock, I cannot regale you with valid footplate experiences from the days of steam. All I can do is reminisce about the lines, men and locomotives met and visited in those closing years. It is fortunate indeed that so many of those at the sharp end of the years of steam are able to recount their experiences. Happily, the cross-country lines in their final years attracted many admirers and created as much interest as many main lines. As my aim is to try to ally my photographs to my text, a chapter like this strains both resources and memory. Having mentioned the Somerset and Dorset however, my strength fails in the attempt not to write the odd paragraph or two on this most loveable of lines.

What more is there to write about the S & D? Born in 1862 from fusion of the Somerset Central Railway and the Dorset Central Railway, the main line of the new company was established, a year later, from Burnham-on-Sea to Wimborne, whence S & D trains connected with the London and South Western line to Poole on the south coast. As the LSWR laid down its lines to and through Bournemouth, a cross-country link was created that, strangely, touched many points in my life – alas too late. Either I

PLATE 58. A very rare photograph: Stanier '8F' 2–8–0 No. 48662 approaches Didcot off the DNS line, on 17 July 1965. (See page 128.)

was blissfully unaware of what I was missing, or by the time realisation arrived, the line had gone. My wife Jane's family come from Burnham-on-Sea: my Nanny was born in Wimborne: my publishers are in Poole: and we live just along the coast, at the end of the LSWR Lymington Branch!

The greatest recorder of the S & D must surely be Ivo Peters. Many of the top railway photographers 'worked' on the line. The scarcity of colour photographs of the S & D is, I suppose, no more marked than the accepted paucity of colour material generally from steam's declining years. Although my efforts were geographically mainly restricted to the Highbridge area they remain amongst my fondest memories. S & D purists understandably insist that the imposition by Western Region of GWR motive power on the Highbridge Branch following WR takeover of the line and its inevitable closure, was not only an insult but a curse, because their engines were unsuitable. It is not my intention here to enter into this debate. Enough is it for me pictorially to recall the presence on the line of GWR motive power. Having failed to gain control of the line in 1876 the GWR and their like-minded heirs on Western Region determined to close it at an early date, so their motive power was in use only as long as it took them to wreak their revenge.

129

My first sight of the S & D was at the tailend of 1962. By then that fateful change of regional boundaries in 1958, which gave Western Region dominant control of the line, had begun to ring the changes which were so soon to become a death-knell. In December 1962, '2251' class 0–6–0 No. 2219 looked not out of place inside Highbridge shed. A few weeks later I again saw Ivatt 2–6–2T No. 41304 on shed there, awaiting duty on the Bason Bridge milk train.

At this time there was an old GWR push-pull coach outside the shed, which I photographed deliberately with Brent Knoll in the distant background. For me and for untold tens of thousands there will never be another line like the S & D, even though I barely knew it, and remember it not at all in its heyday.

My last visit with camera to the line was on 20 February 1965. Although a bleak winter's day, combined with the grime and decline of the line, militated against colourful photography, my fifteen shots that day endure as a cherished record. In spite of everything they had endured, the remaining staff determined to keep the place alive, if they could. But it was not to be.

The month before my final pilgrimage to Highbridge, I had been at Guildford for the final weekend of steam on the SECR Reading-Guildford-Redhill line. From Guildford ran the former

PLATE 59. Eastleigh's BR/Std Class '4' 2–6–0 No. 76060 zips smartly through Botley with an Eastleigh to Fratton freight on 14 July 1965. A mere five months later this engine will have been withdrawn, stored for a few weeks at Eastleigh and then hastened to her graveyard: Cohens of Morriston. (*above*)

PLATE 60. S & D purists will reject my view that Collett's '2251' Class 0–6–0s seemed suited to the lightweight passenger services on 'The Branch' between Highbridge and Evercreech Junction. No. 3210 prepares to depart from Highbridge S & D on 18 August 1963 with the 16.00 train to Templecombe and (Saturdays only) Wincanton. Truly a cross-country railway scene.

LBSCR cross-country line to Horsham, and Ivatt 2–6–2 tanks were in action here, too. On a marvellous, crisp sunny winter's day, the sight of smoke and steam silhouetted against a clear blue sky seemed both natural and eternal. By day's end it was gone for good from Guildford. The Horsham line stuttered on for a few more weeks, closing on 14 June 1965.

Of those numerous cross-country lines in Scotland, in Wales, in East Anglia – my cupboard is bare. My late arrival on the scene post-dated their early demise. Our countryside is poorer without them. If only more had survived into the era of protest in which we now live, some of today's rent-a-crowd might have been able to mobilise themselves usefully in favour of keeping something old, instead of railing against anything new.

PLATE 61. Another nostalgic S & D scene at Highbridge. As this branch was originally the main line, the station covered a considerable area, and had five platforms, although two of the dead-end platforms served only one line, as can be seen here. With the closure of the Burnham line to regular passenger trains in 1951, the station, relegated to branch status as long ago as 1874, became almost a ghost station. Imposition of GWR motive power in the last few years of its life deeply offended the older staff on the branch. On a gloomy winter day, 20 February 1965 – just a year before final closure – '57xx' 0–6–0PT No. 4631, with single coach and one van, blasts out of Highbridge with the 16.00 train to Evercreech Junction.

12 Kitson, Ree and Milne

Did you ever ponder the feelings of Ralph Assheton, sandwiched between Pronghorn and Jairou? Or yet Miles Beevor, placed as he was between Falcon and Merlin? I suppose there is untapped potential for railway quiz or crossword on this theme. Giving names to individual railway engines is as old as *Rocket* or *Morning Star*. I have not researched to discover who was the first *person* to have an engine named after him: it almost certainly was a male, although *Boadaecia* made it quite early on.

Locomotive classes often became known, indeed were created to be known as a class to which connected names were attached. Over the years the Great Western diligently and successfully pursued this theme, from the first *Morning Star* – there were three – to *Evening Star* itself, the last steam locomotive to be built in Britain, at Swindon naturally. The themes pursued by the Great Western tended to be less personal than those employed by other railways. 'Star's and 'Counties', 'Castle's, 'Hall's and 'Grange's spring to mind; although the most powerful locomotives were the 'King's. Naturally over the years the GWR named engines after its more eminent men, particularly of the earlier years. Brunel, Gooch, Dean, Churchward all had their rightful memorial. Although the LNER created *A.H. Peppercorn* (60525) in December 1947 whilst the man himself was Chief Mechanical Engineer, neither Collett nor Hawksworth was similarly honoured by the Great Western.

A cursory study of the techniques of naming locomotives seems to place them into seven categories. There was the 'Good & the Great', like the 'King' Class. There was the 'Geographical', naming towns, cities, schools, historic buildings and so forth, often located within the operational sphere of the relevant railway. Then there was the 'Legendary', taking names extracted from great anecdotes, ranging from biblical to modern times. Another category might be entitled 'Sporting', featuring racehorses or football teams. Next we have 'Patriotic', featuring

names of regiments, naval ships or battles – one's that we won, of course! Naturally and properly there was a category for the 'Men of the Railway' world, such as are featured in this Chapter's title. Another rough heading could be 'Natural history'; included here would be, perhaps animals noted for their speed.

Having said that, we would need to include an eighth category: 'miscellaneous'. Indeed some engines were given weird names, not always either attractive or explicable. One ponders over 'Snake', or indeed 'Viper'.One strange quirk of fate concerns the ill-destiny that attended classes named after rivers. The Highland Railway 4–6–0s and Maunsell's 2–6–4 tanks come to mind.

One wonders what name was used on more engines than any other? Was any name used by each of the 'Big Four'? Who were some of the more obscure people after whom some engines were titled? And what about the internal 'railway politics' surrounding the naming process? The Billinton 'D3's naming sequence must have been traumatic. A class of 0–4–4T introduced in 1892 they were named, as was the prevailing custom on the London, Brighton & South Coast Railway (LBSCR). No. 363 was named *Goldsmid*; No. 364 *Truscott*; thereafter all the remaining engines – there were thirty-six built – were named, without exception, after places on the LBSCR. Indeed in July 1895 No. 363 became *Havant*, leaving *Truscott* very much the odd one out, until, quite early on in their lives the whole class lost their names when repainted in new colours. The name '*Goldsmid*' reappeared in June 1895 on an LBSCR 'B2' class 4–4–0.

The naming of locomotives was a conscious act of personalisation, in an era when it was normal practice for drivers to have their 'own' engines. William Stroudley, Locomotive Superintendent of the Highland Railway 1865–9, and of the LBSCR from 1870 until 1889, in a paper he read to the Institution of Civil Engineers in March 1885, noted that 'if an engine was made as carefully as possible, it would respond to the attention it got afterwards; that the driver would be proud of its appearance and of the duty he could get out of it; and doubly proud to be able to perform a great duty with a small amount of expense'.

He further noted 'It was to be found that the same man would not take the care of another engine, should he have to work one for a time, as he did of his own; and those engines which had unfortunately to be entrusted to several drivers deteriorated in quality, consumed more coal, and got dirty and out of repair much more rapidly than those which were appropriated to particular men.'

These are not the dreamy thoughts of a railway enthusiast, but the considered views of a man responsible for running a railway.

135

Indeed, Stroudly believed that it would be financially worthwhile for a railway company to have one engine per driver, because the additional capital cost would be offset by reduced stores and maintenance charges. Thus the naming of locomotives had as much to do with economics and industrial relations, as it had with cosmetics. However, the realisation of the publicity value of named locomotives, grew with the passage of time. Increased sophistication of motive power was accompanied by increased sophistication of public relations techniques.

By the time of the Grouping, the marketing practices of the Big Four were well developed. Generally speaking, names were given only to those locomotives that were certain or likely to be hauling passenger trains. This practice was continued until the end of steam: thus the 'Britannia's were named, the '9F' 2–10–0s were not – with one exception in each case. (I never did discover why 70047, alone amongst the 'Britannia's, never received a name. I asked Mr Riddles the reason for this, and he could not tell me.)

Since the dawn of the railway age, it has been assumed that eulogy and veneration were reserved for the glamorous express passenger locomotives, rather than the humble goods engine: thus the practice of naming the former, during steam's heyday. Who could imagine named panniers or 'Jinties'? Notwithstanding my personal predilection for ancient, nameless and anonymous small engines during my six years search for steam, one could not help but be attracted to the 'namers'. Strangely though, or perhaps not so strangely, the GWR practice of designating classes with names, such as 'Hall's or 'Counties', copied in later years by LMS and SR, seemed more to personalize their locomotives. Even today, fifty years on, *KGV* is *KGV*, whilst *Flying Scotsman* is 4472 to many true enthusiasts: perhaps because the LNER did not designate its locomotive classes by name.

That having been said, the naming of locomotives after senior railway management was an excellent manifestation of the 'personality cult'. Imagine what might be achieved today if motor-cars, or lawn-mowers were given class names of managers of trades union officials! Now, left as we are with detailed records of the great age of steam, we can but ponder the personality, the life-style of Messrs Kitson, Ree & Milne. Sir Frank Ree, as a former General Manager of the LNWR, was honoured by the naming of LMS 'Patriot' Class No. 45530: Sir James Milne, a former General Manager of the Great Western, has his memorial in 'Castle' Class No. 7001. Although there was a W Kitson, locomotive superintendent of the Great Eastern Railway 1865–6, and the same name was attached to the small class of 0–4–0 ST introduced by the LMS in 1932, and described as 'Kitson design prepared to

PLATE 64. Appropriate for this chapter. LNER 'B1' 4–6–0 No. 61237 *Geoffrey H. Kitson* moves cautiously into Derby shed and on to the turntable, on 9 September 1966. (The naming policy of the LNER for the 'B1's is described on page 140).

Stanier's requirements for LMS': my title is taken from LNER 'B1' No. 61237, named after an LNER director at the time of nationalisation.

Rightly in my view, many of the directors of the Big Four felt the need to perpetuate the individuality and character of their shortly-to-be-deceased companies, immediately prior to nationalisation. Thus, as the LNER ceased to exist on 31 December 1947 the directors gave themselves the satisfaction of perpetuating their names on eighteen 'B1' 4-6-0s during that month, one of whom was Geoffrey H Kitson (see p. 139). Owing to the length of some of the names, all seventeen sets of nameplates had smaller lettering than the forty 'antelope' names on the 'B1's. Originally, incidentally, it was intended to name only those 'B1's built by the LNER in the company's workshops. In order, however, to achieve their laudable ambition the directors naming decision meant that some of the 'B1's built by the North British Locomotive Co. and one built by Vulcan Foundry, during the last six months of the LNER's existence, broke their initial intention.

Numerous cases have been recorded of names of engines being changed, withdrawn or switched. I told the tale of 'School's Class No. 30923 (née Uppingham) in *In Search of Steam*. Royal events, breakdowns and failures, exhibitions and numerous miscellaneous occurrences caused expediency to obtain preferment over consistency. One of the less well-known examples concerned 'B1' No. 61379 (see page 103), *Mayflower*. Attached to its side were plaques stating: 'This locomotive was named Mayflower 13 July 1951 as a symbol of the ties between the two towns of Boston and of the lasting friendship between the USA and the British Commonwealth'. Chartered on 4 October 1959 to carry a trainload of American tourists from King's Cross to Boston, 61379 ran her axleboxes hot on the journey from her Immingham base up to King's Cross. Unable to rectify the damage in time, King's Cross turned out 'B1' No. 61179, suitably renumbered 61379 with nameplates fitted: surely a case of deception being acceptable to alleviate disappointment.

The naming of engines was occasionally less than welcome. Personally I was offended by BR Southern Region's use of the names of erstwhile 'King Arthur' class locomotives on their allocation of BR Standard '5MT' 4-6-0s. *Iseult* looked fine I am sure on a clean green express; but on a scruffy once-black engine the tiny name-plate looked at best incongruous. The sight of a named '5MT' left me totally unmoved.

I can however, recall with nostalgic pleasure, the sight of certain 'namers'. For some reason Thompson LNER 'A2/3' No. 60523 *Sun Castle* became a particular chum. Perhaps because I had least contact with the LNER, and thus took far fewer

PLATE 65. A handful of people, places or events leave an indelible mark on one's memory as one journeys through life. My recent visit to China brought me into intimate contact with Emperor Qin Shi Huang, who first unified China, in 221 BC. I shall always remember him; so too do I recall Thompson class 'A2/3' 4-6-2 No. 60523 *Sun Castle*. Built in August 1947, I saw this engine three times only, yet for some reason her memory is indelible – like Qin Shi Huang. Here, *Sun Castle* threads the tracks in that strange railway hinterland in the vicinity of Top Shed, King's Cross. Note the signal gantry at right centre background, the North London line on the over bridge, and that distinctive structure bearing the word *EBONITE*.

photographs, my meetings with *Sun Castle* have remained with me. My first shot of her was perchance one of my first colour photographs: it was from the platform-end of King's Cross Station in November 1962. Indeed, my records tell me she was the first named engine that I photographed. The following March we met again, in that remote railway world that existed in the vicinity of Top Shed (see plate 64). Our last tryst was on 7 July 1963. *Sun Castle* was withdrawn, on the scrapline at Peterborough New England shed. She has long since departed this life, but I shall not forget her.

13   Yorkshire

To seek to encompass an area as large and important as Yorkshire within a single chapter may seem an infernal cheek. For some strange reason it seems that my railway reading, and certainly my own movements during the steam era, have been concentrated more on Lancashire, so conscience dictates that I redress the balance. Much railway coverage of Yorkshire dwells extensively on the passage through the County Palatine of the Great Northern Railway (GNR) main line. Glance at any book of the great railway photographers and names like York and Doncaster spring constantly from the pages: but by the mid-sixties, GN main-line steam was in decline, so searching for steam in Yorkshire meant getting off the beaten track. Before reading further please accept my apology for paucity of 'Yorkshire' material.

As steam on former LNER territory was being eliminated more rapidly than on the LMS lines, my time and disposition were thus self-allocated towards the latter. Therefore, as Sales Director of the May Fair Hotel, and subsequently attached closely to Sir (then Mr) Maxwell Joseph, my travels north from London to almost anywhere other than the remaining steam strongholds, were invariably dictated by commercial necessity. The purchase by one of his companies of a small hotel in Wakefield necessitated a visit there September 1965. This was unfamiliar territory for me, and time was strictly limited. On the same day I managed to fit in a visit to Goole. No disrespect is intended to Goole or to Wakefield in suggesting that neither place, in 1965, seemed likely to yield vivid visions of LNER steam at its zenith. The precise delineation of the boundary between Eastern and North Eastern Region was unknown to me until the information was deliberately sought. In fact, the North Eastern Region was merged into an enlarged Eastern Region on 1 January 1967, with headquarters at York. Thus, my excursion to Goole and Wakefield on 14 September 1965 became the second of the only two photographic visits made to North Eastern Region territory.

The memory of that day still remains strong. Wakefield was cooling towers, red-brick shed and coal trains, in a framework of railway trackwork spreading north and south, east and west. Goole was long, straight, grey. Memory mingles with fact once one comes to write anecdotes; the facts contained in my precious record book. Strange indeed is the feeling , almost reincarnation, as the Ian Allan *abc* is consulted. Even the cover of this invaluable tool of reference is beginning to tell its own tale, by the date in question. From *abc BRITISH RAILWAYS LOCOMOTIVES* in the 'Winter 1962/63 Edition', has been dropped both the 'abc' and the date some three editions later. Perhaps 'abc' was too unsophisticated. Certainly from the marketing viewpoint, removal of the date from the front of the book must have increased the stockable shelf-life of the books. However, the experienced purchaser of the 'combined volume' knew the importance of turning immediately to the page at the front headed NOTES ON THE USE OF THIS BOOK. At the bottom was the vital information giving the dates, for each BR region, to which the 'numbers of steam locomotives in service have been checked'. In front of me now as I write is the edition in which North Eastern Region locomotive information is accurate up to 6 November 1965. My visit to Wakefield and Goole was 14 September 1965. Some readers hopefully will appreciate the pleasure of checking my photographic record against the detail in my Ian Allan 'Combined Volume'.

Perusing again the front covers of these old Combined Volumes, another subtle yet significant change is apparent as between the '62/63 edition, and that of autumn '65. On the latter, after the word LOCOMOTIVES are added the words AND OTHER MOTIVE POWER. The day of the d.m.u. has dawned, dreary, dull, damnable. I am sorry – you have been dragged a long way from Yorkshire. Let us return to Wakefield and Goole.

My eight colour photographs at Wakefield (56A) that day include shots only of 'B1's and WD 'Austerity' 2–8–0s in action, as well as 'B1's dead on shed. Also dead is a Fowler '4MT' 2–6–4T. The locomotives photographed, in an all-too-brief visit were:

WD	2–8–0	No. 90135	On coal train
B1	4–6–0	61387	Dead on shed
B1	4–6–0	61161	Dead on shed
4MT	2–6–4T	42406	Dead on shed
WD	2–8–0	90642	On shed
WD	2–8–0	90155	On coal train
B1	4–6–0	61289	On coal train
WD	2–8–0	90233	Coupled together, LE
B1	4–6–0	61385	

PLATE 66. Long rakes of coal wagons were an inevitable part of the Yorkshire scene. 'B1' 4–6–0 No. 61289, a long-time resident of Hull Dairy-coates MPD, trundles past Wakefield shed on 14 September 1965. The dolly oppposite the water-column in the background was the point at which Tom Garner, now Secretary of Hordle Branch of the Christchurch and Lymington Conservative Association, used regularly to hitch a lift on a light engine. No. 61289 was one of the last surviving 'B1's, being withdrawn in June 1967.

The mere act of writing their details has set me on the road to seeking what happened to these engines. It is late October 1980: some sixteen years since my visit to Wakefield Shed. All around me as I write, are the reference books of the 'trade'. Delving into numerous railway journals from the past I am soon lost in a nostalgic trip. One is indeed grateful to those numerous and anonymous observers, whose information is quite invaluable and completely irreplaceable. Legion were their ranks. Prosaic was their prose. Their efforts re-read bring back the bitter-sweet pangs of the decline of steam. As the months slip by, the recorded appearances of steam dwindle. *Railway Observer* December 1967 records:

'DONCASTER. Apart from a daily trip from Royston steam is virtually non-existent here . . .'

At Farnley Junction we read:

'The coaling tower still remained at the time of writing'.

At 'LOW MOOR – A visit on the day after closure, 2nd October, revealed twenty steam engines present, all dead.'

145

Of Wakefield and Goole, little is written. Details of the decline and fall of the 'Austerity' 2–8–0s are scarce. Unnoticed in their prime and unloved in their decline, these workhorses, so much a feature of the Yorkshire scene, slipped from the stage more with stealth than with acclaim. No. 90135, an Ardsley engine at the time I photographed her at Wakefield, was transferred to Sunderland (52G) in December 1966. Here she remained, to become one of the very last 'Austerities' to be withdrawn, from Sunderland in September 1967. Nos. 90155 and 90233 were Wakefield (56A) engines, at home at the time of my visit. No. 90155 survived at Wakefield until January '67: 90233 was withdrawn in May that year. No. 90642 had been on Ardsley's (56B) books immediately prior to my visit, but was transferred to Wakefield in the September. She was transferred to Normanton in January 1967. Her last reported sighting, more or less intact, was on 14 April 1968, standing dead at the closed shed at Wakefield, awaiting scrapping.

As late as 24 March 1967 it was reported that, of seventy-one locomotives at Wakefield Shed, only ten were diesel: yet in August 1967 *Railway Observer* did not list Wakefield as one of the remaining sheds with any steam allocation. Of the engines, dead and withdrawn at the closed shed on 9 July 1967, only 90233 remained of the four 'Austerities' seen on my visit. Of the four 'B1's that I had recorded back in September 1965 there was no sign. For details of their demise I am indebted to Mr P B Hands. No. 61161, a Wakefield engine, was withdrawn therefrom in December 1966. No. 61289 was allocated to Hull (Dairycoates) (50B) and 61385 to Ardsley (56B) at the time I photographed them at Wakefield, as recorded. No. 61289 was one of the few 'B1's to survive into 1967, being withdrawn in June that year. No. 61385, and Wakefield's own 61387 were both withdrawn officially in the month after I photographed them.

'B1's and Yorkshire were synonymous. On Great Northern, North Eastern and Great Central lines in the county they were a familiar sight from their introduction in 1942. In later years they spread into the former LMS lines. The very first engine built, LNER No. 8301 *Springbok* was completed and sent to Doncaster for official inspection on 13 December 1942, entering traffic six days later. Eventually totalling over 400 engines, the class required no major development, which speaks for itself. The 'B1' was Edward Thompson's most significant contribution to British locomotive practice and performance: some would say his only contribution of merit: but that is another story.

The 'B1's as a class remained intact until November 1961, at which date 207 of the 409 engines were 'maintained' at Doncaster. No. 61289 was one of the batch ordered and built by

PLATE 67. Allocated to Goole MPD (50D) in July 1965, Ivatt '4MT' 2–6–0 No. 43077 simmers on her home shed, on 14 September 1965. The next month her brief sojourn at Goole was terminated by transfer to Royston (55D). Note the lamps awaiting positioning before the next turn of duty.

the LNER, but not finally put into traffic until February 1948, when it was given the prefix E before its number, prior to the BR numbering scheme's introduction. Of all the sheds to which 'B1's were allocated, probably the largest number was at Sheffield (Darnall) which, at 31 December 1961 had forty-four members of the class. Doncaster had a good number allocated, so did York in the later years. Yorkshire 'B1's were used on almost all types of passenger and freight work. The West Riding allocation was frequently used on excursion and summer Saturday trains. They were traditionally used on the Rugby League Cup Final trains to London. Bradford's 'B1's were regular performers twixt their home base and Wakefield at the head of the Bradford portion of the King's Cross expresses.

By June 1965, just before my rare visit to photograph steam in Yorkshire, there were only fifty-six 'B1's left in active service in the North-Eastern Region, with the majority in Yorkshire: Ardsley had fourteen, Dairycoates seven, Low Moor seven, Wakefield twelve and York ten. This accounted for most of the class, which became extinct from former North Eastern Railway sheds in June 1967. As mentioned earlier, 61289 was one of the final survivors.

In answer to your question 'why is he going on so much about the "B1"s,' I have to confess to finding too few opportunities to write about LNER motive power, and my time, albeit very brief, at Wakefield gives me the excuse. At Goole, later on 14 September 1965 I took just four photographs. In spite of the place's NER heritage, there was not an LNER engine in sight. The four photographs taken comprised:

WD	2–8–0	No. 90072	On mineral train
4MT	2–6–0		43077	On shed, in steam
WD	2–8–0		90091	On shed, in steam
4MT	2–6–0		43098	Inside shed, in steam

Of the two 'Flying Pigs', 43077 seems to have had a varied life-style. Having spent some years at Hull (Dairycoates) MPD, she appears briefly to have been transferred to Goole (50D) in July 1965. I saw her there, before transfer away, this time to Royston (55D) in October. In February 1967 she moved again, to Manningham (55F), from where she was withdrawn in May. Stored thereafter at Wakefield, she was finally cut up at Drapers, Hull in August 1967: truly a Yorkshire engine. The other Ivatt 'Pig', 43098 had a long sojourn at Goole, but was transferred away the month after my photograph, to Normanton, where she remained until withdrawn in June 1967. She too was then stored at Wakefield after which I cannot trace her demise.

The departure of the 'Flying Pigs' from Goole left the

PLATE 68. End of steam, end of an era in Yorkshire. Sadly, few bothered to record, in colour, the death-throes of engine-sheds once teeming with activity, and historic buildings borne of the industrial revolution. On 25 July 1967, from the window of a Leeds to Manchester train, I photographed Farnley Junction MPD soon after closure, and not long before demolition. On the right is the shed's lodging-house, used mainly by King's Cross enginemen 'overnighting' after working trains from King's Cross to Leeds. It was demolished with the shed, which was a twelve-road unit built by the LNWR in 1882 and designed to hold sixty engines.

'Austerities' more or less in sole command as allocated steam: by May 1967 the seven members of the class were all that remained of Goole's steam stock. No. 90091 was still there. As *Railway Observer* noted in January 1967:

'GOOLE – An average of eight steam-hauled mineral and goods trains pass this station during daylight, mostly worked by Dairycoates and Goole WDs, with one turn worked by Wakefield on which a variety of engines have been used.'

If lack of personal detail about, and photography in, Yorkshire causes annoyance at this chapter's title, my apologies are freely given. There is little else for me to offer. A few minutes was all I could spare on a fleeting visit to Leeds on 28 March 1963. At City Station I was fortunate to photograph Peppercorn 'A1' Pacific No. 60155 *Borderer* receiving final attention from her crew before departure on a passenger train. Also, shunting vans, I captured Fowler 2–6–4T No. 42409. No. 60155 was blowing-off vigorously, the fire in the firebox is just visible, and one of the station's splendid water-columns is to the fore. Sadly, both shots are on Gevacolour, which must be the worst colour-film I ever used. Not only is the colour poor, the film has faded very badly, albeit kept in the same conditions as my other transparencies.

My only other catalogue entries in Yorkshire occurred on 25 July 1967, and in appalling photographs illustrate the demise of steam. However, the act of writing about them has at last solved one of the very few mysteries surrounding the location of one of my pictures. In a nutshell, my dilemma was simple: 'was it Copley Hill or Farnley Junction?' Thanks to my need to find the solution before putting anything in this book, and thanks even more to the detailed information and photographs in *LMS Engine Sheds* by Chris Hawkins and George Reeve, the problem is solved at last – it is Farnley Junction. Taken from a passing train in rotten light, the end-product is recognizable, albeit utterly depressing. The weeds have already taken over the track area. Gone was the activity, the life, the steam. Ghosts of LNWR days must already haunt the twelve-road shed, which closed on 26 November 1966. Designed to accommodate sixty engines, it stood in the fork of the Farnley and Dewsbury lines. Coded 55C on transfer to the North-Eastern Region in October 1956, its last years hosted a large stud of WD 'Austerity' 2–8–0s, as well as five 'Jubilee's to work the main passenger trains to Lancashire, whence I was *en route* that day. To the end, Farnley Junction shed provided motive power for important trains to Lancashire, including 'Jubilee' 45562 *Alberta* on the 21.45 Leeds to Stockport parcels on the day before the shed's final closure.

One steam engine was all that Yorkshire yielded on that dismal day. Near Mirfield, and from the window of my diesel-hauled train I fired off my Voigtlander twice at '8F' 2–8–0 No. 48166. The combination of rotten light, filthy engine and moving subject and photographer produced an unprintable result.

My final photograph of Yorkshire's steam heritage, before plunging into the Stygian gloom of Standedge Tunnel that July day in 1967, was of another deserted shed. Huddersfield's Hillhouse MPD opened in the first half of the nineteenth century. Notwithstanding reported closure in the early 1960s it struggled on, officially closing on 2 January 1967 but still remaining as a signing-on point until 5 November. Thus ended well over one hundred years of distinguished and fruitful mechanical and human history.

By the end of 1967, steam engines working to and through Yorkshire were becoming very scarce. They bore shedplates from Lancashire. The few steam-hauled freights through Standedge Tunnel – the route of the LNWR main line between industrial Lancashire and Yorkshire – were hauled mainly by LMS 'Black 5's and '8F's. The famous 'Friday's Only' Manchester Exchange to York was steam-hauled for the last time on 29 December 1967, by 'Britannia' 4–6–2 No. 70013 *Oliver Cromwell*: the last BR steam

PLATE 69. If it is true that a prophet is without honour in his own country, it is equally true that little notice was taken of, and even less affection lavished on steam work-horses fulfilling their designated role in familiar surroundings. Thus an 'Austerity' 2–8–0 on a freight working in Yorkshire was photographically unfashionable. No. 90072 trundles a lengthy rake of empty wagons past Goole Mineral Junction on 14 September 1965.

In the background the former L & Y line crosses the line from the docks, on which 90072 is travelling. It would appear to be some time since the track was ballasted.

engine to be overhauled at Crewe. The Preston Mail from Huddersfield was steam-worked for the last time on the previous day.

By April 1968 *Railway Observer* noted poignantly 'It is still possible to see a steam locomotive in Sheffield.' Only just: detailing the movement, light-engine, of an '8F' from Heaton Mersey MPD (9F) is like searching for food on a plate that has been through an efficient washing-up machine. The occasional 'steamers' still trundled into the county from Lancashire, notably the Carnforth-Skipton goods many miles away, but the end was nigh ... Demolition of Hillhouse shed, site of my last photograph, commenced on May Day 1968: by 24 May – formerly Empire Day – the site was levelled ... There is nothing more to write. The demise of Yorkshire steam seems to have coincided with the decline of Yorkshire cricket ...

14   31871 (75B)

We first met at Redhill in April 1963. It was in the early days of my photography, when the call of steam was barely audible. Indeed it was my first visit to Redhill Shed. For an ill-informed enthusiast Redhill was an odd place, so it seemed, to have an engine-shed. Redhill to me, was merely a place avoided by fast trains on the London-Brighton main line. I was unaware of the Tonbridge-Redhill-Guildford-Reading services. 'S15's and 'Q1's at the shed, in company with 31871, led me to suppose that Redhill was a freight-engine shed. Chapter 9 in my previous book *In Search of Steam* details the educational process by which I learned about the South Eastern and Chatham (SECR) line to Reading.

No. 31871 lived at Redhill. Born in July 1925 she was a 'Woolworth', one of the Maunsell 'N' class Moguls built at Woolwich Arsenal with government funds to alleviate unemployment and subsequently purchased by the SR. That day in April 1963 was the first of a number of meetings in what it transpired was to be her last year of life, for she was withdrawn at the end of the year, and was scrapped at Eastleigh works in January 1964.

No. 31871 was transferred to Redhill MPD from Bricklayers Arms Shed in May 1959. For this information I am indebted to Mr P B Hands, whose astonishing series *What Happened to Steam* first appeared in 1980. It is a self-evident tribute to the lasting interest in steam, that Mr Hands should have spent seven years of intensive research discovering, documenting and publishing the shed-allocations of literally thousands of steam engines during the last ten years of steam on BR. The call of steam manifests itself in many ways, so this chapter simply records my casual contact with one engine, first photographed in April and finally seen in October 1963.

That first photograph (Plate 70) was of course experimental. Steam engines do not look their best when photographed standing on top of them.

PLATE 70. This photograph perhaps shows more about Redhill's coaling-plant than about the subject of this short chapter. An 'S15' 4–6–0 is taking coal in front of 31871. (*left*)

PLATE 71. Even in her swan-song 31871 was kept in fairly good condition externally, and was given charge of inter-regional trains. The driver leans well out, rounding a curve twixt Dorking and Gomshall and Shere on 20 July 1963.

Soon this line will play an important role as a 'London By Pass' to the Channel Tunnel. No. 31871 was a long-time resident of Redhill MPD. She was finally cut-up at Eastleigh in January 1964. (*above*)

On 20 July 1963, Driver Abbott had charge of 31871, entrusted with the 08.45 through train from Margate to Wolverhampton and shown on page 64 of *In Search of Steam*. She seemed in good condition. Later that day she was still active on passenger duty, as I duly photographed her near Dorking, again in charge of an inter-regional train, this time comprising Western Region stock. My final photograph, and not a very good one, was on 10 October. Still active on passenger duty, she had charge of the 15.04 Redhill to Reading (Southern) train.

Redhill shed was finally closed in June 1965 when steam was displaced from the Reading-Redhill service. By then the shed had become the last remaining steam depot on Southern Region's Central Division. It had been in existence for over a century. In its declining years, the depot's principal passenger duties were connected with the SECR cross-country line. Redhill was the only point on the line at which reversal was necessary. Although a 65 ft turntable and modern coal stage were provided in 1928, the SR never fulfilled their plan to replace the old shed building. Apart from an asbestos roof fitted by BR in 1950, the shed structure remained unaltered. Designated 75B in its latter years, the shed was in the fork of the Tonbridge and Brighton lines, south of Redhill Station.

No. 31871's withdrawal was occasioned more by management's decision to introduce new BR Standard motive power, than by evidence of exhaustion of the Maunsell 'Mogul's. They were such versatile locomotives that, properly maintained, they would still be giving satisfactory service. Their performance on the inter-regional trains, especially those entering GWR territory at Reading, was not one whit inferior to the more celebrated, and much more modern 'Manor' class.

'Manor's were frequent visitors to Redhill: but they were not the only 'foreign' visitors. Occasional 'Black 5's and 'B1's appeared, too. My photographic sessions at Redhill yielded 'S15', 'Q', and 'Q1', as well as 'N' and 'U' classes in April 1963. On 13 April No. 7813 *Freshford Manor* was on shed.

Photographing one engine in different locations became like meeting a friend unexpectedly. Those who engineered the removal of steam from Britain's railways, foreclosed a very happy chapter of my life.

PLATE 72. With Barry town in the background, two long-term inmates of Dai Woodham's scrapyard on 13 July 1981 prepare for a new lease of life. Filling the foreground is Churchward 2–8–0T 4248, from a class introduced before the First World War. On the right, 'Modified Hall' 4–6–0 No. 5967 *Bickmarsh Hall* has begun to receive care and attention for the first time since withdrawal from Westbury MPD in June 1964. Over the years, Barry's sea air has eroded much paint, to reveal the BR 'Lion & Wheel' emblem on 4248's tank-side. (*below*)

15   Barry

PLATE 73. 6984 *Owsden Hall*
was built in February 1948
and withdrawn at the death
of GWR steam, in December
1965; a mere stripling. Quite
frantic allocation and re-
allocation in her last two
years on BR active service,
could not of course prevent
the inevitable. Between
September 1963 and April
1965, 6984 was transferred
from Worcester MPD to
Severn Tunnel Junction to
Cardiff Canton to Neath back
to Severn Tunnel Junction
and finally to Bristol Barrow
road. Condemned to Barry
Docks in February 1966, few
could have imagined this
photograph being taken more
than 15 years later.
(*below*)

As preservationists – be they realists or dreamers – continue their dramatic rescue of the surviving engines in Dai Woodham's scrapyard at Barry in South Wales, I end this book with a reminder of this place that has become as Mecca to two generations of Britain's railway enthusiasts.

Confidently I predict that between the writing of these words, and the publication thereof, yet more Barry engines will have left the graveyard of despair for another home: a home of hope, somewhere. . . .

Abbreviations

BR	—	British Rail
BR/Std	—	British Rail Standard Classes of locomotives
CME	—	Chief Mechanical Engineer
Caley	—	Caledonian Railway
d.m.u.	—	Diesel multiple-unit
DNS	—	Didcot Newbury & Southampton Railway
e.c.s.	—	Empty carriage stock
e.m.u.	—	Electric multiple-unit
G & P	—	Glasgow & Paisley Joint
G & SW	—	Glasgow & South Western Railway
GC	—	Great Central Railway
GN	—	Great Northern Railway
GNS	—	Great North of Scotland Railway
GWR	—	Great Western Railway
HR	—	Highland Railway
HST	—	High-speed train
KGV	—	*King George V*
LBSCR	—	London Brighton & South Coast Railway
LE	—	Light engine
LMS	—	London Midland & Scottish Railway
LNER	—	London & North Eastern Railway
LNWR	—	London & North Western Railway
LSWR	—	London & South Western Railway
MGN	—	Midland & Great Northern Railway
MPD	—	Motive Power Depot
MR	—	Midland Railway
MSW	—	Midland & South Western Junction Railway
MT	—	Mixed Traffic engine classification
Mogul	—	Locomotive of 2–6–0 wheel-arrangement
NB	—	North British Railway
NE	—	North Eastern Railway
PPW	—	Portpatrick & Wigtownshire Joint Railway
PT	—	Pannier tank
Pacific	—	Locomotive of 4–6–2 wheel-arrangement
RCTS	—	Railway Correspondence & Travel Society
S & DJR	—	Somerset & Dorset Joint Railway
SECR	—	South Eastern & Chatham Railway
SR	—	Southern Railway
T	—	after wheel-arrangement, denotes tank-engine
WD	—	War Department (engines built under Government auspices during the Second World War, subsequently sold into BR stock and classified WD)

Index

It is *not* intended to index every place, event or locomotive mentioned in the text. The post-grouping 'Big Four' are not indexed, to avoid repetition: nor are the British Rail regions, or BR itself.

Generally, people and places relevant to the photography and narrative, are included. The photographs, charts and maps are referred to in bold type.